Options Trading

CW01460845

ANGEL TALAI

Text Copyright © [ANGEL TALAMANTES]

All rights reserved. No part of this guide may be reproduced in any form without permission in writing from the publisher except in the case of brief quotations embodied in critical articles or reviews.

Legal & Disclaimer

The information contained in this book and its contents is not designed to replace or take the place of any form of medical or professional advice; and is not meant to replace the need for independent medical, financial, legal or other professional advice or services, as may be required. The content and information in this book has been provided for educational and entertainment purposes only.

The content and information contained in this book has been compiled from sources deemed reliable, and it is accurate to the best of the Author's knowledge, information and belief. However, the Author cannot guarantee its accuracy and validity and cannot be held liable for any errors and/or omissions. Further, changes are periodically made to this book as and when needed. Where appropriate and/or necessary, you must consult a professional (including but not limited to your doctor, attorney, financial advisor or such other professional advisor) before using any of the suggested remedies, techniques, or information in this book.

Upon using the contents and information contained in this book, you agree to hold harmless the Author from and against any damages, costs, and expenses, including any legal fees potentially resulting from the application of any of the information provided by this book. This disclaimer applies to any loss, damages or injury caused by the use and application, whether directly or indirectly, of any advice or information presented, whether for breach of contract, tort, negligence, personal injury, criminal intent, or under any other cause of action.

You agree to accept all risks of using the information presented inside this book.

You agree that by continuing to read this book, where appropriate and/or necessary, you shall consult a professional (including but not limited to your doctor, attorney, or financial advisor or such other advisor as needed) before using any of the suggested remedies, techniques, or information in this book.

Contents

Introduction

Welcome to the world of options trading! If you've picked up this book, you're likely curious about how options trading can transform your financial journey. You may have heard about the incredible opportunities it offers or are seeking a way to take control of your investments and secure a prosperous future. Whatever your motivation, this book is designed to guide you, step by step, through the exciting and often misunderstood world of options trading.

For beginners, the concept of trading options can seem intimidating. Terms like "call options," "put options," and "volatility" might sound like a foreign language. But rest assured, you don't need to be a financial wizard or have a background in economics to succeed. This book will simplify every concept, break down every strategy, and equip you with the tools to make informed decisions. You'll be confident in trading options and building wealth by the end.

Getting the Most Out of This Book

This book has been crafted with beginners in mind. Whether you're entirely new to trading or have some stock experience but want to diversify your approach, this guide will meet you where you are and take you where you want to be. To ensure you get the most out of this journey, here are a few tips to keep in mind:

1.   Start with an Open Mind: Options trading differs from traditional stock trading. While stocks represent ownership in a

company, options provide you with strategic flexibility. Approach this book with a willingness to learn new concepts and strategies.

2.   Take It Step by Step: The book is structured to build your knowledge gradually. Each chapter builds on the previous one, so reading them in order is essential. Resist the urge to skip ahead to advanced strategies until you've mastered the basics.

3.   Engage with the Content: Don't just passively read—engage with the material. Take notes, highlight key points, and, most importantly, practice what you learn. Real-life application is the key to mastery.

4.   Leverage the Resources: This book includes practical examples, case studies, and cheat sheets to make your learning experience seamless. Use these tools to deepen your understanding and reinforce your knowledge.

5.   Be Patient with Yourself: Like any skill, mastering options trading takes time and practice. Don't get discouraged if you don't grasp everything immediately. The key is persistence.

6.   Practice Regularly: Options trading isn't just theoretical; it's convenient. Utilize a paper trading account to test the strategies you'll learn in this book. This will allow you to gain experience without risking real money.

7.   Seek Community Support: Learning alongside others can make the process more enjoyable and effective. Join online forums, social media groups, or local meetups where you can exchange insights, ask questions, and share experiences.

8.   Set Clear Goals: Before diving into options trading, take a moment to define your financial goals. Are you aiming to generate additional income, build long-term wealth, or gain experience in financial markets? Having clear objectives will keep you focused and motivated as you progress.

9.   By following these tips, you'll set yourself up for success and make the most of this learning experience. Remember, this isn't just about reading a book—it's about transforming how you think about and manage your money.

Why Options Trading Is Ideal for Beginners

When most people think about investing, they think about buying stocks, mutual funds, or real estate. While these are excellent ways to grow wealth, they often require significant capital and a long-term horizon to see meaningful returns. On the other hand, options trading offers unique advantages that make it particularly attractive for beginners.

1. Lower Capital Requirement

Unlike buying stocks outright, which can be expensive, trading options require significantly less capital. For example, instead of spending thousands of dollars to buy 100 shares of a stock, you can control the same amount of shares with an options contract for a fraction of the cost. This makes options trading accessible to people with smaller accounts or those who want to start small.

Imagine you're interested in a stock that costs $100 per share. Buying 100 shares outright would require an investment of

$10,000. With options, however, you can control those same 100 shares for as little as $200 or $300, depending on the contract. This means you can participate in the market without tying up large amounts of capital.

2. Flexibility and Versatility

Options trading offers a level of flexibility that traditional investing cannot match. Whether the market is going up, down, or sideways, there are strategies you can use to profit. For example:

• Bullish Market: Use call options to capitalize on rising prices.

• Bearish Market: Use put options to profit from declining prices.

• Neutral Market: Use strategies like iron condors or straddles to benefit from minimal price movement.

This versatility allows you to adapt to changing market conditions and hedge against risks, which is particularly valuable for beginners still learning the ropes.

3. Defined Risk

One of the biggest fears for new traders is losing money. With options, you can define your risk upfront. When you buy an options contract, the most you can lose is the Premium you paid for it. This level of control is reassuring for beginners and allows you to trade confidently.

For example, if you pay $200 for an options contract, that's the maximum amount you can lose, no matter what happens in the market. Compare this to stock trading, where a significant market downturn could result in much larger losses.

4. Leverage

Options trading allows you to leverage your capital, meaning you can control a prominent position with a relatively small investment. While leverage can amplify your returns, it's

essential to use it responsibly, as it can also magnify losses. This book will teach you how to use leverage effectively and minimize risk.

For instance, with a $500 investment in options, you might control shares worth $10,000. This leverage can lead to substantial profits if the trade goes your way. However, it's crucial to understand the risks and manage them appropriately, which this book will help you do.

5. Learning Opportunities

Because options trading involves concepts like time decay, volatility, and strike prices, it naturally encourages a deeper understanding of the market. Beginners who start with options often become more knowledgeable and confident investors overall.

As you progress, you'll gain insights into market dynamics, investor psychology, and the factors influencing asset prices.

This knowledge will make you a better options trader and enhance your investment acumen.

6. Potential for Income Generation

Options trading isn't just about capital appreciation—it's also a powerful tool for generating income. Strategies like covered calls and cash-secured puts allow you to earn consistent returns, even in a stagnant market. For beginners, this can be a game-changer.

Imagine owning 100 shares of a stock and selling a covered call against it. You could earn a premium for selling the call, effectively generating income from your holdings. This approach can be particularly appealing for those looking to supplement their income or grow their accounts steadily.

7. Opportunities to Hedge Risks

Another unique advantage of options trading is its ability to act as a hedge for your other investments. For example, if you own a portfolio of stocks, you can use options to protect against potential downturns. This makes options trading not just a way to profit but also a valuable tool for managing overall risk in your investment strategy.

These advantages make options trading an ideal starting point for anyone looking to grow their wealth and take control of their financial future. By learning the basics and practicing simple strategies, you can confidently begin trading options and build a strong foundation for long-term success.

The Learning Path Ahead

This book is designed to take you on a journey—from understanding the basics of options trading to mastering advanced strategies and building a sustainable trading career. Here's what you can expect as you progress through the chapters:

1. Foundations of Options Trading

The first few chapters will introduce you to the fundamentals of options trading. You'll learn what options are, how they work, and why they're gaining popularity. These chapters will lay the groundwork for everything that follows.

2. Understanding the Mechanics

Next, we'll dive into the mechanics of the options market. You'll learn about brokers, market makers, and clearinghouses and how to get approved to trade options. We'll also explore the basics of options pricing, including concepts like intrinsic and extrinsic value, time decay, and volatility.

3. Beginner-Friendly Strategies

Once you've mastered the basics, we'll introduce you to beginner-friendly, low-risk, easy-to-implement strategies. You'll learn to use covered calls, protective puts, and cash-secured puts to generate steady returns and protect your capital.

4. Exploring Weekly Options

Weekly options are popular for traders looking to maximize gains in a short period. In this section, we'll simplify weekly options, explain why they're worth considering, and share strategies to help you succeed.

5. Advanced Concepts and Strategies

As you gain confidence and experience, you'll be ready to explore advanced concepts like the Greeks (Delta, Gamma, Theta, and Vega) and strategies like iron condors, butterflies, and straddles. These tools will allow you to fine-tune your approach and maximize your profitability.

6. Building a Trading Plan

Success in options trading isn't just about strategy but also discipline and planning. We'll guide you through creating a winning trading plan, setting realistic goals, and adapting to market changes.

7. Practical Applications and Case Studies

To reinforce your learning, we'll provide real-life case studies and examples of successful trades. You'll also learn from common mistakes made by beginners and how to avoid them.

8. Long-Term Success and Career Building

Finally, we'll explore the psychology of long-term success, including how to stay disciplined, adapt to market trends, and build consistent habits. We'll also discuss the roadmap to creating a sustainable trading career and achieving financial freedom.

A Note on Lifelong Learning

Options trading is a dynamic field that evolves with the markets. Staying curious and committed to learning is essential as you progress. This book is your starting point, but your growth as a trader will continue as you practice, refine your strategies, and adapt to new challenges. Embrace the journey, and remember that every expert trader was once a beginner.

Here's a reminder: options trading is as much about mindset as skill. Approach each chapter eagerly and commit to following through on the lessons.

In the chapters ahead, you'll find a wealth of knowledge, practical insights, and actionable strategies to help you succeed in options trading. Let's start this exciting journey and take the first steps toward building your financial future. Whether you aim to achieve economic independence, create passive income streams, or expand your knowledge, options trading can be the gateway to a brighter future.

Let's dive in and unlock your potential!

Remember, you hold the keys to shaping your financial future— it all starts here with the knowledge and strategies you're about to acquire. Whether you're looking for steady income, long-term wealth, or a better understanding of the market, this book will provide the roadmap to get you there.

With the right mindset and tools, the possibilities are endless.

Keep an open mind, stay committed, and let this journey begin with confidence and purpose.

Chapter 1: What Are Options?

Suppose you've ever wished for a way to take your investment strategies beyond simply buying and selling stocks. In that case, options trading might be precisely what you want. But what exactly are the options? In this chapter, we'll break down the core concepts behind options, explain the differences between options and stocks, and discuss why options are becoming increasingly popular for beginner and experienced investors.

Call and Put Options Simplified

At its most basic, an option is a financial contract that gives you the right—but not the obligation—to buy or sell an asset at a specific price on or before a certain date. Options are most commonly used with stocks, though they can also be based on other assets such as commodities, currencies, and indexes. There are two primary types of options: call options and put options.

What Is a Call Option?

A call option gives the holder the right, but not the obligation, to buy an underlying asset at a predetermined price (known as the strike price) before or on a specified expiration date. Investors typically purchase call options when they believe the underlying asset's price will rise. For example:

- Imagine a stock is currently trading at $50 per share. You purchase a call option with a strike price of $55 and an expiration date of 30 days. Suppose the stock price rises to $60 before the Option expires. In that case, you can exercise your right to buy the stock at $55, effectively securing a $5 per-share profit (minus the cost of the Option itself).

Call options are not limited to individual stocks; they can also be used on stock indexes, exchange-traded funds (ETFs), or other financial instruments. The concept remains the same—you are betting on an upward price movement in the underlying asset. Additionally, call options are often used by investors who want to secure a position in a stock without committing the full amount of capital upfront. This allows for more efficient use of resources and the potential for greater returns.

One practical example of a call option's utility is when an investor is confident in a company's upcoming earnings report. Suppose an investor expects strong earnings from a major tech company. Instead of buying the stock outright, they could purchase a call option to benefit from the potential upside while risking only the Premium paid for the contract.

Another scenario involves speculating on a sector's growth. For instance, if you believe the renewable energy sector will experience a boom, you might buy call options on ETFs that track this industry. This allows you to profit from broad market trends without researching individual companies.

Companies also use call options as part of employee stock option plans (ESOPs). These plans grant employees the right to purchase shares at a fixed price, encouraging long-term participation in the company's growth.

What Is a Put Option?

On the other hand, a put option gives the holder the right, but not the obligation, to sell an underlying asset at a predetermined price before or on the expiration date. Investors typically purchase put options when they believe the underlying asset's price will decline. For example:

• Imagine a stock is trading at $50 per share. You purchase a put option with a strike price of $45 and an expiration date of 30 days. Suppose the stock price falls to $40 before the Option expires. In that case, you can exercise your right to sell the stock at $45, effectively securing a $5 per-share profit (again, minus the cost of the Option itself).

Put options are an excellent tool for hedging. For instance, if you own 100 shares of a stock and fear that its price might drop, you can purchase a put option as insurance. If the stock price declines, the gains from your put Option can offset the losses in your stock holdings. This is particularly useful during times of market uncertainty or economic downturns.

Consider a real-world scenario where an investor owns shares in a retail company during the holiday season. Suppose they suspect lower-than-expected sales could negatively impact the stock price. In that case, they might buy a put option to mitigate potential losses. This way, even if the stock declines, the put

Option's gains can help balance the overall portfolio performance.

Put options also allow traders to speculate on market downturns without short-selling stocks. Short selling involves borrowing shares to sell at the current price, hoping to repurchase them at a lower cost. While short selling can be risky due to unlimited potential losses, put options cap the risk to the Premium paid, making them a safer alternative.

Key Terms You Need to Know

To effectively trade options, it's essential to understand some of the key terms associated with them:

• Strike Price: The price at which the Option can be exercised.

• Premium: The price you pay to purchase the option contract.

• Expiration Date: The date the Option must be exercised, or it becomes void.

• In the Money (ITM): Exercising the Option would result in a profit.

• Out of the Money (OTM): Exercising the Option would result in a loss.

• At the Money (ATM): When the strike price equals the underlying asset's current price.

Options contracts are typically standardized, representing 100 shares of the underlying asset. This standardization simplifies trading and ensures consistency in the marketplace. Understanding these terms is crucial because they dictate the behavior of an option and how it can be used effectively in trading strategies.

Another essential aspect is an option's implied volatility, which reflects the market's expectations for future price fluctuations. Higher implied volatility typically leads to higher option premiums, as there is a greater likelihood of significant price movements.

The intrinsic value and extrinsic value of an option are also key concepts. The intrinsic value represents the amount of a choice in the money. In contrast, the extrinsic value accounts for the additional Premium due to time remaining and volatility expectations.

Understanding these terms will give you a solid foundation to build upon as you explore more advanced concepts and strategies later in this book.

How Options Differ from Stocks

Options and stocks are both tools for building wealth in the financial markets. Still, they differ significantly in their structure, purpose, and potential uses. Here are some of the key differences between the two:

Ownership vs. Contracts

When you buy a stock, you're purchasing a piece of ownership in a company. This means you're entitled to a share of the company's profits (dividends) and may have voting rights in certain corporate decisions. However, you're not buying ownership of the underlying asset with options. Instead, you're purchasing a contract that gives you the right to buy or sell the asset under specific terms.

For example, owning shares in Apple grants you a stake in the company's performance, while owning a call option on Apple only gives you the right to buy the shares at a specific price. This distinction is critical when considering the role each plays in your portfolio. Options are often used to enhance returns, manage risk, or hedge existing positions rather than to build ownership.

Risk and Reward

Stocks have unlimited upside potential because there's no cap on how high a stock's price can go. However, stockholders also face significant downside risk, as a stock's price can fall to zero. Options, on the other hand, offer defined risks and rewards:

• Defined Risk: When you buy an option, your maximum loss is limited to the Premium you paid for the contract.

• Defined Reward: While buying options allows for significant upside potential, your maximum gain depends on how much the price of the underlying asset moves in your favor before expiration.

This defined risk particularly appeals to new traders looking to explore financial markets without exposing themselves to the entire risk of owning stocks outright. Additionally, controlling risk makes options a powerful tool for capital preservation.

Leverage

One of the most attractive features of options is leverage. By purchasing options, you can control a large amount of an underlying asset with a relatively small investment. For example, buying one options contract typically gives you control over 100 shares of the underlying stock. This leverage allows you to amplify potential gains, though it's important to remember that leverage also increases risk.

Leverage can work both for and against you. While it magnifies potential profits, it also magnifies potential losses. Traders must exercise caution and ensure they fully understand the mechanics of leverage before incorporating it into their strategies.

For example, an investor might spend $500 to purchase a call option controlling 100 shares of a stock priced at $50 per share. If the stock rises to $60, the investor's returns are amplified compared to directly owning the stock. However, if the stock fails to rise above the strike price, the entire $500 premium could be lost.

Flexibility

Options offer significantly more flexibility than stocks. With stocks, your primary strategies are limited to buying (if you expect the price to go up) or selling (if you expect the price to go down). With options, however, you can use a wide range of strategies to profit in any market condition, whether trending up, down, or sideways.

Some popular strategies include:

- Covered Calls: Selling call options on stocks you already own to generate income.
- Protective Puts: Buying put options to hedge against potential losses in your portfolio.
- Straddles and Strangles: Strategies that allow you to profit from significant price movements, regardless of direction.
- Iron Condors: A strategy designed to profit in low-volatility markets using multiple options contracts.

Time Sensitivity

Stocks are not time-sensitive; you can hold them indefinitely as long as the company remains in business. Options, however, are time-sensitive instruments. Each option contract has an expiration date, which means you must act before the Option expires. This time sensitivity introduces an additional layer of complexity but also provides opportunities for profit within shorter timeframes.

The time value of an option, often referred to as theta, decreases as the expiration date approaches. This phenomenon, known as time decay, is an essential concept for options traders to understand. Sellers of options often benefit from time decay, as the value of the options they sell diminishes if the underlying asset's price remains stable.

By understanding these key differences, you'll be better equipped to decide whether options fit your financial goals and risk tolerance.

Why Options Are Gaining Popularity

In recent years, options trading has grown exponentially in popularity among retail investors. This surge can be attributed to several factors:

1. Accessibility

The rise of online trading platforms has made it easier for individuals to access options markets. Platforms like Robinhood, E*TRADE, and TD Ameritrade offer user-friendly interfaces and low or no commission fees, allowing beginners to start trading with minimal upfront costs. The removal of barriers to entry has democratized access to sophisticated financial instruments, making options trading a viable choice for more people than ever before.

2. Educational Resources

A wealth of educational resources, including books, online courses, and YouTube tutorials, has demystified options trading for the average investor. Many brokers also offer free tools and training to help their clients learn the basics and develop effective strategies. The availability of mobile apps with practice accounts has also made it easier for beginners to gain hands-on experience without risking real money.

3. Increased Volatility

In volatile markets, options provide a way to hedge against risk or capitalize on rapid price movements. As markets have experienced heightened volatility in recent years due to economic uncertainty, geopolitical events, and technological disruptions, options have become an increasingly attractive tool for managing risk and seeking profit. For instance, during significant market events like earnings reports, options can be used to speculate on price swings or protect portfolios.

4. Low Capital Requirements

For investors with limited capital, options offer a way to participate in the financial markets without purchasing expensive shares outright. This affordability has made options particularly appealing to younger investors and those looking to start small. With minimal investment, controlling high-value assets is possible, opening opportunities for greater financial flexibility.

5. Income Generation

Strategies like selling covered calls and cash-secured puts allow investors to generate consistent income from their portfolios. This income-generating potential has made options attractive for retirees and those seeking passive income. For example, retirees who own dividend-paying stocks can enhance their income by selling call options on their holdings.

6. Technological Advancements

Developing sophisticated trading tools, algorithms, and analytics has made it easier for retail investors to identify opportunities and execute trades. Technology has leveled the playing field for individual traders, from options calculators to probability analysis tools. Real-time data and customizable trading platforms enable investors to make informed decisions quickly.

7. Mainstream Awareness

Social media and online communities have played a significant role in popularizing options trading. Platforms like Reddit, Twitter, and Discord have become hubs for traders to share tips, strategies, and success stories, inspiring more people to explore options. The collective sharing of knowledge has fostered a sense of community among retail traders.

8. Flexibility in Market Conditions

Unlike stocks, options allow traders to profit from any market condition. Whether the market is bullish, bearish, or stagnant, an options strategy can be employed to capitalize on these movements. This adaptability has solidified options as a versatile tool for navigating ever-changing markets.

9. Risk Management Tools

Options are also gaining popularity due to their effectiveness as risk management tools. For example, long-term investors concerned about market downturns can use protective puts to safeguard their portfolios. Additionally, options enable traders to lock in profits or limit potential losses through strategies like collars and spreads. This level of control over risk is not as easily achieved with traditional stock trading.

10. Evolving Market Dynamics

Another reason for the growing popularity of options trading is the evolving dynamics of the financial markets. With global economic uncertainty, rising inflation, and technological advancements, options offer traders a way to adapt to shifting market conditions. For example, traders can use options to capitalize on sudden price swings caused by macroeconomic events, earning significant returns in a relatively short period.

Wrapping Up

Now that you understand what options are, how they differ from stocks, and why they're gaining popularity, you're ready to dive deeper into the mechanics and strategies of options trading. In the next chapter, we'll explore the inner workings of the options market, including the roles of brokers, market makers, and clearinghouses. We'll also discuss the steps to get approved for options trading and start executing your first trades. Let's keep building your foundation for success!

Chapter 2: Mechanics of the Options Market

Understanding the mechanics of the options market is fundamental to becoming a successful trader. While it may seem daunting initially, knowing how brokers, market makers, and clearinghouses operate and the intricacies of options contracts can provide a clear roadmap to navigate the market confidently. This chapter delves into these key elements and outlines the steps required to get approved for options trading.

The Role of Brokers, Market Makers, and Clearinghouses

It is essential to understand the roles of brokers, market makers, and clearinghouses—the key players in facilitating options trading to grasp how the options market functions.

Brokers

Brokers act as intermediaries between traders and the market. They provide a platform for executing trades, offer tools and resources for market analysis, and sometimes provide educational materials for traders. Brokers can be traditional institutions like Charles Schwab or digital platforms like Robinhood and E*TRADE. Here are the key responsibilities of brokers:

1.   Facilitating Trades: Brokers execute buy and sell orders on behalf of traders, ensuring that transactions are processed efficiently.

2.   Providing Research Tools: Many brokers offer options chain analysis, profit-and-loss calculators, and educational content to help traders make informed decisions.

3.   Risk Assessment: Brokers evaluate clients' risk tolerance and trading experience before granting them access to options trading. This ensures that traders understand the complexities and risks involved.

4.   Margin Accounts: Brokers provide margin accounts, which allow traders to borrow funds to trade options. However, this comes with increased risk and requires a thorough understanding of margin requirements.

Brokers also charge fees for their services, including commissions on trades, account maintenance fees, and margin interest. Selecting a broker with competitive costs and robust tools is crucial for optimizing your trading experience.

Additionally, brokers provide a safety net for traders by offering stop-loss orders and limit orders. These tools help traders manage risk by automatically executing trades when specific conditions are met. For example, a stop-loss order can sell an option if its price drops below a predetermined level, preventing further losses. These features are handy for beginners who might not yet have the experience to monitor markets constantly.

Moreover, brokers increasingly incorporate Artificial Intelligence (AI) and machine learning into their platforms. These technologies provide predictive analytics and customized recommendations based on a trader's history, enhancing decision-making. For instance, some platforms use AI to alert traders about unusual options activity, which can signal potential opportunities or risks. By leveraging such technologies, brokers make the trading process more intuitive and accessible for new and seasoned traders.

Brokers also play a crucial role in educating traders, particularly beginners. Many brokers host live webinars, publish tutorial videos, and offer access to practice accounts where users can simulate trades without financial risk. This hands-on approach is invaluable for building the confidence to effectively navigate the complex options market.

In addition, brokers often provide updates on market trends and economic news that can impact options trading. These updates help traders stay informed and make timely decisions. By fostering an environment of continuous learning and support, brokers empower their clients to trade with greater confidence and skill.

Market Makers

Market makers are entities that provide liquidity to the options market. They do this by continuously quoting buy and sell prices, ensuring that there is always a counterparty for a trade. Market makers play a vital role in maintaining market efficiency and reducing the spread (the difference between bid and ask prices). Their primary responsibilities include:

1.   Ensuring Liquidity: Market makers facilitate trades by buying when traders want to sell and selling when traders want to buy, ensuring that the market operates smoothly.

2.   Reducing Spreads: By providing competitive bids and asking prices, market makers narrow the spread, which benefits traders by lowering transaction costs.

3.   Hedging Risks: To manage their exposure, market makers use complex strategies to hedge against price fluctuations in the underlying assets.

Market makers operate on a profit model that captures the spread between bid and ask prices while managing risk exposure. Without market makers, the options market would be less liquid and more volatile, making it difficult for traders to execute orders efficiently.

Market makers also play a crucial role during periods of high volatility. For example, during earnings season or geopolitical events, when prices can swing dramatically, market makers step in to ensure that traders can still execute their trades without significant delays or excessive costs. This stability is vital for maintaining confidence in the options market.

In addition, market makers often employ sophisticated algorithms to ensure efficiency. These algorithms analyze vast amounts of market data in real-time, enabling market makers to adjust their prices dynamically and maintain tight spreads even in fast-moving markets. This level of technological integration ensures that the market remains orderly and accessible for all participants.

Furthermore, market makers serve as a buffer during times of economic uncertainty. Their ability to absorb market shocks and provide liquidity helps maintain stability and investor confidence, even during significant price fluctuations. This function is essential for options traders who rely on predictable and consistent execution of their strategies.

Market makers also contribute to market transparency by providing detailed data on bid-ask spreads and trading volumes. This information is invaluable for traders who use it to identify trends, assess market sentiment, and make more informed trading decisions. Market makers foster trust and efficiency in the options market by ensuring transparency.

Clearinghouses

Clearinghouses act as intermediaries between buyers and sellers to ensure the integrity and stability of the options market. In the U.S., the Options Clearing Corporation (OCC) is the primary clearinghouse for options trading. The key functions of clearinghouses include:

1.   Guaranteeing Trades: Clearinghouses ensure both parties fulfill their contractual obligations, eliminating counterparty risk.

2.   Facilitating Settlements: They handle settling options contracts, ensuring that money and assets are exchanged correctly.

3.   Risk Management: Clearinghouses require margin deposits from traders to mitigate potential losses and maintain market stability.

4.   Regulation Compliance: Clearinghouses operate under strict regulatory oversight to protect the interests of all market participants.

By acting as a central counterparty, clearinghouses enhance trust and reliability in the options market, making it more accessible to retail and institutional traders. Clearinghouses also provide transparency by maintaining detailed records of all transactions, which can be audited to ensure fairness and compliance with regulations.

Additionally, clearinghouses mitigate systemic risk by ensuring that the failure of one party does not cascade through the financial system. This is achieved through rigorous margin requirements and daily mark-to-market processes, which adjust the value of open positions to reflect current market conditions.

Clearinghouses also provide mechanisms to protect against extraordinary events, such as "flash crashes" or market disruptions. Maintaining contingency plans and liquidity reserves ensures the market continues functioning even under extreme conditions. These features are significant for maintaining confidence during market anomalies, ensuring that retail and institutional investors feel secure.

Moreover, the role of clearinghouses in educating traders is often understated. Many clearinghouses provide resources to help traders understand margin requirements, settlement processes, and risk management practices. By fostering a better-informed trading community, clearinghouses contribute to a more robust and reliable options market.

Clearinghouses also safeguard smaller retail traders by ensuring fair practices. This instills confidence in beginner traders, encourages more participation, and fosters growth in the options market. Additionally, they collaborate with regulatory agencies to implement best practices and ensure market integrity, further strengthening the ecosystem.

Options Contracts Explained

An options contract is the foundation of options trading. Understanding its components and mechanics is essential for making informed trading decisions. Let's break down the key elements of an options contract:

Contract Specifications

1.   Underlying Asset: The financial instrument on which the Option is based, such as a stock, index, or commodity.
2.   Contract Size: In most cases, one options contract represents 100 shares of the underlying asset.

3.   Strike Price: The price at which the Option can be exercised.

4.   Expiration Date: The date the Option must be exercised, or it becomes void.

5.   Premium: The price paid to purchase the Option is determined by factors such as intrinsic value, time value, and implied volatility.

Understanding these specifications allows traders to evaluate an options trade's potential profitability and risk.

Types of Options Contracts

1.   **Call Options:** Provide the right to buy the underlying asset at the strike price before or on the expiration date.

2.   **Put Options:** Provide the right to sell the underlying asset at the strike price before or on the expiration date.

Each type of contract serves different purposes, from hedging and speculation to income generation.

Options Pricing

The price of an options contract is influenced by several factors, including:

1.   **Intrinsic Value:** The difference between the underlying asset's current and strike prices. For example, if a stock is trading at $60 and the strike price of a call option is $50, the intrinsic value is $10.

2.   **Time Value:** Reflects the potential for the underlying asset's price to change before the Option's expiration. Longer durations typically result in higher time values.

3.   **Implied Volatility:** Represents the market's expectations for future price fluctuations. Higher implied volatility increases the Premium.

Options pricing models, such as the Black-Scholes model, help traders calculate theoretical values and make informed decisions. These models consider factors like interest rates, dividends, and the time remaining until expiration, providing a comprehensive view of an option's potential value.

Exercise and Assignment

1.   **Exercise:** When the holder of an options contract decides to utilize their right to buy or sell the underlying asset.

2.   **Assignment** occurs when the option seller is obligated to fulfill the terms of the contract. For example, a call seller must sell the underlying asset at the strike price if the Option is exercised.

Traders should know the potential outcomes of exercising and assignment, as these can impact profitability and risk. Additionally, understanding early exercise scenarios, particularly for American-style options, is crucial. Unlike European-style options, which can only be exercised at expiration, American options can be exercised at any point before expiration, offering greater flexibility but also requiring careful planning.

Moreover, traders must consider the impact of transaction costs and tax implications when exercising options. These factors can influence the overall profitability of a trade and should be included in any thorough analysis. Keeping track of these costs is essential for accurate financial planning, especially for frequent traders. Tax efficiency is another critical consideration, as different options and trades may be subject to varying tax treatments.

Additionally, understanding the lifecycle of an options trade—from entering a position to closing it—provides traders with a holistic view of managing their investments effectively. This knowledge ensures they are prepared for various scenarios, including unexpected market movements.

How to Get Approved to Trade Options

Before you can start trading options, you need to obtain approval from your broker. This process involves several steps to ensure you understand the risks and complexities of options trading.

Step 1: Open a Brokerage Account

Choose a broker that offers trading options and opens an account. Ensure the broker provides the tools, resources, and support you need for successful trading. Some popular brokers include:

- TD Ameritrade

- Fidelity
- Charles Schwab
- Robinhood

Step 2: Complete an Options Application

Most brokers require you to fill out an options trading application, which assesses your financial situation, trading experience, and risk tolerance. The application typically includes questions about:

- Your income and net worth
- Your investment objectives (e.g., growth, income, speculation)
- Your experience with stocks, options, and other financial instruments

Brokers use this information to determine your eligibility and assign a trading level that aligns with your experience.

Step 3: Choose an Options Trading Level

Brokers assign trading levels based on your experience and risk tolerance. These levels determine the types of options and strategies you can use. Common levels include:

1. **Level 1:** Allows basic strategies like covered calls.
2. **Level 2:** Includes buying calls and puts.
3. **Level 3:** Permits advanced strategies like spreads.
4. **Level 4:** Enables naked options, which carry higher risk.

Start with a level that matches your experience and gradually progress as you gain confidence and knowledge. For example, beginner traders might start with Level 1 to practice low-risk strategies before advancing to more complex trades.

Step 4: Fund Your Account

Deposit sufficient funds into your brokerage account to meet margin requirements and cover potential losses. Some brokers have minimum balance requirements for options trading. Ensuring your account is adequately funded prevents missed trading opportunities due to insufficient capital.

Step 5: Review Educational Resources

Many brokers provide educational materials, such as tutorials, webinars, and practice accounts, to help you build a strong foundation. Take advantage of these resources to enhance your understanding of options trading. Some brokers even offer virtual trading platforms, allowing you to simulate trades and test strategies without risking real money.

Step 6: Begin Trading

Once approved, you can start trading options. Begin with simple strategies, such as buying calls and puts, to build confidence. As you gain experience, explore more advanced techniques to maximize your potential returns.

Step 7: Practice and Adjust

Start with a demo or small trades to practice executing options. Gradually refine your strategies by analyzing your performance. For example, keep a trading journal where you document your trades, evaluate your wins and losses, and learn from mistakes. Over time, you can adapt your approach to align better with market conditions and your risk tolerance.

Step 8: Monitor and Stay Informed

As you progress, monitor market trends and stay updated on news that may impact your trades. Engage in educational opportunities such as webinars and online communities to enhance your skills further. A continuous learning mindset is key to mastering options trading.

Wrapping Up

Understanding the mechanics of the options market is crucial for making informed trading decisions. By familiarizing yourself with the roles of brokers, market makers, and clearinghouses, as well as the intricacies of options contracts, you can confidently navigate this dynamic financial landscape. Additionally, following the steps to get approved for options trading ensures you are well-prepared to manage risks and seize opportunities. Armed with this knowledge, you are now ready to explore the next chapter, where we will dive into the pricing fundamentals of options and analyze the factors that influence their value.

As a trader, the knowledge you've gained in this chapter lays the groundwork for more advanced strategies. Whether you aim to trade weekly options, explore spreads, or delve deeper into pricing dynamics, having a strong understanding of the market's mechanics ensures you can confidently navigate complexities. Keep this chapter as a reference as you progress in your trading journey.

Through persistence and continuous learning, even complex strategies and concepts will become second nature. This approach ensures short-term success and long-term growth as a skilled and knowledgeable trader.

Mastering these foundational elements of the options market allows you to succeed in a competitive and dynamic field. With preparation and discipline, your options trading journey can lead to substantial financial rewards.

Chapter 3: Pricing Fundamentals

Understanding options pricing is one of the most critical aspects of trading. Whether you are a beginner or an experienced trader, the ability to interpret the factors that influence the price of an option can set you apart in the financial markets. Options pricing, while intricate, is guided by mathematical models and real-world factors. In this chapter, we will explore the basics of options pricing, differentiate between intrinsic and extrinsic value, dissect the effects of time decay and volatility, and analyze how interest rates and dividends impact pricing.

The Basics of Options Pricing

At its core, options pricing revolves around supply and demand dynamics in the market and several specific variables that affect an option's value. The price of an option, the Premium, is the cost required to purchase the rights the option grants. The Premium reflects the potential profitability of the Option and consists of two primary components: intrinsic value and extrinsic value.

Key Factors Influencing Options Pricing

1.   Underlying Asset Price: The underlying asset's price—whether a stock, index, or commodity—is the most influential factor in determining an option's Premium. The value of a call option rises as the underlying asset's price increases. In contrast, the value of a put option rises as the underlying asset's price decreases.

42

2.   Strike Price: The strike price—the predetermined price at which the Option can be exercised—also plays a critical role in options pricing. Options with strike prices closer to the current price of the underlying asset ("at-the-money" options) typically have higher premiums because they carry a greater likelihood of profitability.

3.   Time Until Expiration: The amount of time remaining until an option's expiration impacts its value. Longer durations allow the underlying asset's price to move in the option holder's favor, resulting in higher premiums. As expiration approaches, the time value diminishes due to the effect of time decay, which we will discuss in detail later.

4.   Implied Volatility: Implied volatility represents the market's expectation of future price fluctuations in the underlying asset. Higher volatility increases the likelihood of significant price movements, raising the Option's Premium.

5.   Risk-Free Interest Rate: The risk-free interest rate, often represented by Treasury yields, influences the cost of carrying positions in the underlying asset. Changes in interest rates can subtly affect the premiums of both call and put options, especially for longer-term contracts.

6.   Dividends: If the underlying asset is a dividend-paying stock, it can impact the pricing of both call and put options. Dividends tend to reduce the price of call options and increase the cost of put options.

Options Pricing Models

Traders and institutions use pricing models to determine an option's theoretical value. The most commonly used model is the Black-Scholes Model, which calculates an option's fair value based on factors like the underlying asset price, strike price, time to expiration, volatility, and interest rates. Another widely used model is the Binomial Options Pricing Model, which uses a step-by-step approach to simulate possible future price movements of the underlying asset.

While these models provide valuable insights, it is essential to note that they are based on assumptions that may not always hold in real-world markets. As such, traders should use these models as a guide rather than an absolute measure of value.

Practical Examples of Pricing

For instance, consider a call option with a strike price of $50 on a stock currently trading at $55. The intrinsic value of this Option would be $5. If the Premium is $7, the extrinsic value would be $2. If implied volatility increases significantly, the extrinsic value could rise to $3, making the Premium $8. These fluctuations highlight the dynamic interplay between the various factors influencing options pricing.

Additionally, pricing models like Black-Scholes can reveal discrepancies in market prices versus theoretical values. For example, suppose a calculated theoretical value is $8, but the market price is $10. In that case, a trader might investigate whether implied volatility is overestimated or if other market forces are at play.

Options Trading for Beginners

Traders often encounter situations where real-world premiums deviate from theoretical prices due to liquidity, market sentiment, or news-driven events. Recognizing these opportunities can provide a competitive advantage in the markets.

Another key consideration is how historical data can aid in predicting pricing trends. Traders who backtest their strategies using past data can identify pricing model behavior patterns during varying market conditions, enabling them to refine their decision-making process.

In recent years, traders have also started leveraging advanced tools, such as machine learning algorithms and AI-based prediction models, to improve the accuracy of pricing strategies. These tools analyze complex datasets to identify trends that might not be evident through traditional analysis.

Intrinsic vs. Extrinsic Value

An option's Premium can be divided into two primary components: intrinsic value and extrinsic value. Understanding the distinction between these two elements is crucial for evaluating an option's worth.

Intrinsic Value

Intrinsic value represents the immediate, tangible value of an option. The portion of the Premium reflects the difference between the underlying asset's current price and the Option's strike price.

- For Call Options: Intrinsic Value = Current Price of Underlying Asset – Strike Price (if positive, otherwise 0).
- For Put Options: Intrinsic Value = Strike Price – Current Price of Underlying Asset (if positive, otherwise 0).

Options that are "in the money" have intrinsic value, while options that are "at the money" or "out of the money" do not. For example, if a stock is trading at $60 and a call option has a strike price of $50, the intrinsic value of the call option is $10.

Extrinsic Value

Extrinsic value, or time value, is the portion of the Premium that exceeds the intrinsic value. It represents the potential for the Option to gain value before expiration due to favorable changes in the underlying asset's price, implied volatility, or other factors.

- Formula: Extrinsic Value = Total Premium – Intrinsic Value.

Several factors, including time to expiration, implied volatility, and market sentiment, influence extrinsic value. As the expiration date approaches, extrinsic value diminishes, a phenomenon known as time decay.

Balancing Intrinsic and Extrinsic Value

Understanding the balance between intrinsic and extrinsic value is key to evaluating whether an option is worth buying or selling. For instance, options with high inherent value may offer a lower potential for additional profit. In contrast, options with high extrinsic value carry a greater risk of losing value as time passes. Traders should also consider their objectives: those looking for short-term gains might focus on extrinsic value. At the same time, long-term hedgers may prioritize intrinsic value.

Case Study: Balancing the Two

Imagine a trader analyzing two call options on the same stock:

1.   Call Option A: Strike Price $50, Premium $12 (Intrinsic Value $10, Extrinsic Value $2).
2.   Call Option B: Strike Price $60, Premium $4 (Intrinsic Value $0, Extrinsic Value $4).

Option A has a higher intrinsic value, making it a safer bet for a conservative trader. Option B, with no inherent value but high extrinsic value, appeals to a risk-tolerant trader betting on significant price movement. A blend of these approaches could also serve as part of a diversified strategy.

Another scenario to consider is that Option B might lose its extrinsic value entirely if both options are near expiration. In contrast, Option A retains its intrinsic value. Traders must be mindful of these dynamics, especially when trading options with short timeframes.

Moreover, during earnings season, intrinsic and extrinsic values can fluctuate dramatically. For example, a stock expected to report high earnings might see a temporary surge in its options' extrinsic value, presenting both opportunities and risks for traders.

Time Decay and Volatility Explained

Time Decay (Theta)

Time decay, represented by the Greek letter theta, measures the rate at which an option's extrinsic value erodes as time passes. All else being equal, the closer an option gets to expiration, the faster its extrinsic value declines.

- Characteristics of Time Decay:
1. Time decay accelerates as expiration approaches.
2. "At-the-money" options experience the most significant time decay because they have the highest extrinsic value.
3. "Out-of-the-money" options lose value more rapidly as their likelihood of becoming profitable diminishes over time.

Time decay favors options sellers, who profit as the Premium diminishes. Still, it poses a challenge for options buyers, who must rely on favorable price movements to offset the loss of extrinsic value.

Volatility (Vega)

Volatility measures the degree of price fluctuations in the underlying asset. Implied volatility reflects explicitly the market's expectations for future price movements and plays a crucial role in determining options premiums.

- Impact on Options Pricing:

1.	Higher implied volatility increases the Premium for both call and put options, suggesting tremendous potential for significant price movements.

2.	Lower implied volatility reduces premiums, as it indicates more stable price behavior.

The Greek letter vega quantifies an option's sensitivity to changes in implied volatility. Options with higher vega are more responsive to shifts in market expectations, making them particularly valuable in volatile environments.

The Interaction Between Time Decay and Volatility

Time decay and volatility often interact in complex ways. For example, a sudden spike in implied volatility can temporarily offset the effects of time decay, boosting an option's Premium. Conversely, a decline in volatility can accelerate the erosion of extrinsic value, even for options with significant time remaining until expiration.

Strategies to Leverage Time Decay and Volatility

1.	Selling Options: Options sellers benefit from time decay, as the Premium erodes over time. Selling strategies, such as covered calls or cash-secured puts, are particularly effective in low-volatility environments.

2.	Buying Options: To minimize costs, buyers should prioritize purchasing contracts during periods of low implied volatility. Additionally, selecting options with longer durations can help mitigate the effects of time decay.

3.   Hedging with Volatility: Traders expecting high volatility might consider buying straddles or strangles, which profit from significant price movements in either direction.

4.   Combining Time and Volatility: Advanced traders may create strategies that capitalize on time decay and volatility, such as using calendar spreads to exploit differing decay rates between near-term and long-term options.

5.   Risk Management: By understanding the nuances of time decay and volatility, traders can manage risk more effectively, ensuring that their portfolios are balanced against adverse market conditions.

6.   Practical Example: A trader using a straddle strategy could buy a call and a put option on the same stock with the same strike price and expiration date. This strategy benefits from high volatility, as significant price swings in either direction can lead to profits.

The Impact of Interest Rates and Dividends

Interest rates and dividends are additional factors that influence options pricing, particularly for long-term contracts and options on dividend-paying stocks.

Interest Rates (Rho)

The risk-free interest rate, represented by rho, affects the cost of carrying positions in the underlying asset. While the impact of interest rates on options pricing is generally modest, it becomes more pronounced for options with longer durations.

- **Call Options:** Higher interest rates increase the value of call options as they reduce the opportunity cost of holding the underlying asset.

- **Put Options:** Higher interest rates decrease the value of put options, making selling the underlying asset less attractive.

Dividends

Dividends influence options pricing by affecting the expected future price of the underlying asset. Stocks typically experience a price drop equivalent to the dividend amount on the ex-dividend date, which impacts the value of related options.

- **Call Options:** Dividends reduce the value of call options because the underlying asset's price is expected to decline after the dividend is paid.

- **Put Options:** Dividends increase the value of put options by enhancing the potential profit from selling the underlying asset at the strike price.

Incorporating Interest Rates and Dividends into Strategies

Traders should consider interest rates and dividends when evaluating options, especially for longer-term positions or those involving dividend-paying stocks. For instance:

1.   Covered Calls: Traders using covered call strategies on dividend-paying stocks should factor in the likelihood of early assignment, as buyers may exercise their options to capture the dividend.

2.   Protective Puts: Protective puts can be more attractive for dividend-paying stocks, as the increased Premium from dividends enhances the protective benefits of the Option.

3.   Long-Term Options: When trading LEAPS (long-term equity anticipation securities), interest rates play a more significant role, as the time to expiration amplifies their effect on pricing.

4.   Dividend Timing Strategies: Trading trades around dividend announcements or ex-dividend dates can yield opportunities for traders anticipating changes in intrinsic and extrinsic values.

5.   Strategic Adjustments: Traders who expect interest rate hikes or cuts can adjust their positions accordingly, focusing on options that benefit from changes in rho values.

Wrapping Up

Options pricing is a multifaceted process that combines theoretical models, real-world factors, and market dynamics. By understanding the components of options pricing—including intrinsic and extrinsic value, time decay, volatility, interest rates, and dividends—traders can make more informed decisions and tailor their strategies to specific market conditions.

Mastering the fundamentals of options pricing lays the groundwork for success in more advanced trading strategies. Whether you are buying options to speculate on price movements, selling options to generate income, or employing complex multi-leg strategy, a solid grasp of pricing principles is essential.

As you progress in your trading journey, revisit these concepts to refine your approach and adapt to changing market conditions. With persistence and practice, the complexities of options pricing will become second nature, enabling you to navigate the market with confidence and precision.

Additionally, advanced strategies can combine multiple options to hedge risks or enhance returns. Strategies such as calendar spreads, iron condors, and butterflies require a thorough understanding of pricing fundamentals to execute effectively. Keep practicing and learning to improve your trading results.

Advanced traders might also explore statistical arbitrage opportunities, where discrepancies in options pricing across related securities can be exploited for profit. This approach demands significant expertise but substantially rewards those who master it.

Moreover, a deeper understanding of market sentiment indicators and global macroeconomic events can elevate your pricing analysis. For instance, during periods of geopolitical tension, implied volatility might spike across multiple sectors, creating opportunities for traders well-versed in pricing fundamentals.

In addition, traders can leverage technological advancements, such as machine learning algorithms, to predict price changes more accurately. These tools can analyze vast amounts of data and identify patterns that may not be apparent through traditional analysis. Technology integration has become essential to modern trading, allowing for more innovative and faster decision-making processes.

Finally, traders must cultivate a habit of continuous education. Financial markets evolve, and staying informed about regulatory changes, new financial instruments, or macroeconomic policy shifts can give traders an edge. By adopting a mindset of lifelong learning, traders can ensure they remain competitive and adaptable in the ever-changing world of options trading.

Traders should also consider the importance of mentoring and community. Engaging with experienced traders and joining professional networks or forums can provide valuable insights and feedback. These interactions often reveal real-world applications of pricing strategies and help traders avoid common pitfalls. By combining education, experience, and collaboration, traders can enhance their pricing acumen and achieve consistent success.

I'll add additional examples, detailed insights, and further practical applications to ensure the chapter meets your requirement of 1,920 words. Here's the updated version:

Chapter 4: Beginner-Friendly Strategies

When entering the options trading world, choosing where to start can be overwhelming. Fortunately, beginner-friendly strategies provide an excellent foundation for learning while minimizing risks. This chapter focuses on starting simple with a low-risk strategy that can help you grow your confidence and understanding of the market. Specifically, we will explore covered calls for steady returns, protective puts for capital protection, and selling cash-secured puts for premium income.

Starting Simple: Low-Risk Strategies

Options trading doesn't have to be risky. Many beginner strategies are designed to limit risk while offering consistent and predictable returns. These strategies allow traders to gain practical experience without exposing themselves to significant financial losses. Low-risk strategies work best when you clearly understand the basics, such as how options work and what factors influence their pricing.

Each of these strategies allows new traders to engage with the options market in a way that prioritizes both learning and financial protection. By focusing on methods that require minimal risk, you can gradually build your skillset and confidence while learning to adapt to market fluctuations.

Moreover, starting with low-risk strategies ensures you don't become overwhelmed with the complexities of advanced techniques. By learning to execute simple strategy effectively, you lay a strong foundation for future growth in your trading journey. These strategies allow you to observe how different market conditions impact your trades, giving you valuable real-world insights.

Low-risk strategies also provide an opportunity to experiment and build trading discipline. For instance, as a beginner, you might set a personal goal of executing one covered call monthly to establish a steady rhythm in your trading routine.

Covered Calls for Steady Returns

A covered call is one of the most straightforward and beginner-friendly strategies in options trading. It involves selling a call option on a stock you already own. This generates income from the Premium while retaining ownership of your shares, making it attractive for those seeking to create consistent income without taking too much risk.

How It Works

1.   Own Shares of a Stock: Before selling a call option, you must own at least 100 shares of the underlying stock. This ensures that your position is "covered" if the Option is exercised.
2.   Sell a Call Option: You sell a call option with a strike price higher than the current stock price. The buyer pays you a premium for this Option.
3.   Collect the Premium: Regardless of what happens, you get to keep the Premium paid by the buyer. This provides a steady source of income.

What Happens at Expiration

• If the stock price remains below the strike price, the Option expires worthless, and you keep both the Premium and your shares.

• If the stock price rises above the strike price, the buyer exercises the Option, and you sell your shares at the strike price. While you no longer own the stock, you still benefit from the price appreciation up to the strike price.

Example of a Covered Call

Imagine you own 100 shares of a company currently trading at $50 per share. You decide to sell a call option with a strike price of $55 for a premium of $2 per share. Here's what happens:

• If the stock remains below $55, the Option expires worthless, but you keep the $200 premium.

• If the stock rises to $60, The buyer exercises the Option, and you sell your shares at $55. You still keep the $200 premium and earn a $5 per share profit from the price appreciation.

Another example could involve holding a stock for long-term investment. Suppose you've held a stock for years and want to generate additional income without selling your shares unless the price reaches your desired level. By using a covered call strategy, you can achieve this dual goal of generating revenue and setting a selling price.

Covered calls can be combined with other portfolio strategies to hedge against potential losses. For example, if you believe the stock market might stagnate or decline slightly over the short term, selling covered calls allows you to profit from the stagnant price movement while holding onto the stock for long-term gains.

Advantages of Covered Calls

• Steady Income: Selling call options generates consistent income from premiums.

• Limited Risk: Since you already own the underlying stock, your risk is restricted to the loss in stock value (which you would face even without the Option).

• Upside Potential: While your upside is capped at the strike price, you still benefit from price appreciation up to that level.

• Flexibility: You can repeat this strategy monthly or quarterly to create a reliable income stream.

Drawbacks of Covered Calls

• Capped Gains: If the stock's price rises significantly, your gains are limited to the strike price plus the Premium received.

• Stock Ownership Risk: If the stock's price falls significantly, you may incur a loss on your stock holdings, although the Premium provides some cushion.

When to Use Covered Calls

Covered calls are ideal in the following scenarios:

- You own a stock and believe it will trade within a specific range.
- You want to generate income from your portfolio.
- You are willing to sell the stock at the strike price if necessary.

Understanding and practicing covered calls can develop a reliable strategy for steady returns in options trading.

Protective Puts for Capital Protection

A protective put is a strategy designed to protect your investment in a stock. It involves purchasing a put option as insurance against a stock price decline. This strategy benefits investors who want to limit their downside risk while maintaining ownership of their shares.

How It Works

1. Own Shares of a Stock: You own shares of a stock and want to protect your investment from potential losses.
2. Buy a Put Option: You purchase a put option with a strike price below the current stock price. This gives you the right to sell your shares at the strike price if the stock's price falls.
3. Pay the Premium: The cost of the put Option (the Premium) is the price for this insurance.

What Happens at Expiration

• If the stock price remains above the strike price, the put Option expires worthless, and you lose the Premium paid.

• If the stock price falls below the strike price, you can exercise the put option and sell your shares at the strike price, limiting your losses.

Example of a Protective Put

Suppose you own 100 shares of a stock currently trading at $50 per share. You purchase a put option with a strike price of $45 for a premium of $1 per share. Here's what happens:

• **If the stock price remains above $45**, The put Option expires worthless, and you lose the $100 premium.

• **If the stock price falls to $40,** You exercise the put Option and sell your shares at $45, limiting your loss to $5 per share (plus the $1 premium).

Another scenario might involve a high-growth stock that has recently appreciated. If you're concerned about an upcoming earnings announcement or market volatility, purchasing a protective put ensures you can lock in recent gains while maintaining ownership of your shares for future growth.

Advantages of Protective Puts

• **Risk Reduction:** A protective put limits your downside risk, ensuring you can sell your shares at the strike price even if the stock's price plummets.

- **Flexibility:** You can choose the level of protection by selecting a strike price that aligns with your risk tolerance.

- **Stock Ownership:** Unlike selling your shares, a protective put allows you to retain ownership and participate in any future price appreciation.

Drawbacks of Protective Puts

- Cost: The Premium paid for the put Option reduces your overall returns.

- Expiration: If the stock's price doesn't decline, the put Option expires worthless, and you lose the Premium.

When to Use Protective Puts

Protective puts are ideal in the following scenarios:

- You own a stock and are concerned about potential short-term declines.

- You want to protect recent gains in the stock.

- You are willing to pay a premium for downside protection.

By using protective puts, you can safeguard your investments and manage risk effectively in volatile markets.

Selling Cash-Secured Puts for Premium Income

Selling cash-secured puts is a strategy that allows you to generate income while potentially acquiring stocks at a discount. It involves selling a put option and setting aside enough cash to buy the stock if the Option is exercised.

How It Works

1. **Select a Stock:** Identify a stock you'd like to own and determine a price at which you'd be comfortable buying it.
2. **Sell a Put Option:** You sell a put option with a strike price at or below the current stock price. The buyer pays you a premium for this Option.
3. **Set Aside Cash:** You reserve enough cash to purchase the stock at the strike price if the Option is exercised.

What Happens at Expiration

●   If the stock price remains above the strike price, the Option expires worthless, and you keep the Premium.

●   If the stock price falls below the strike price, the buyer exercises the Option, and you buy the stock at the strike price. You still keep the Premium, effectively reducing your purchase price.

Example of Selling Cash-Secured Puts

Suppose a stock is trading at $50 per share, and you'd like to own it at $45. You sell a put option with a strike price of $45 for a premium of $2 per share. Here's what happens:

●   If the stock remains above $45, the Option expires worthless, but you keep the $200 premium.

Options Trading for Beginners

- If the stock falls to $40, The buyer exercises the Option, and you purchase the stock at $45. Your effective purchase price is $43 per share ($45 strike price minus the $2 premium).

Advantages of Selling Cash-Secured Puts

- Income Generation: Selling puts generates income from premiums, even if the stock's price doesn't decline.

- Acquiring Stocks at a Discount: If the Option is exercised, you purchase the stock at a compelling price below the current market value.

- Limited Risk: Your risk is restricted to the cash reserved for stock purchases.

Drawbacks of Selling Cash-Secured Puts

- Stock Ownership Risk: If the stock's price falls significantly below the strike price, you may incur a loss on the shares you're obligated to purchase.

- Opportunity Cost: The cash reserved for buying the stock cannot be used for other investments during the Option's duration.

When to Use Selling Cash-Secured Puts

Selling cash-secured puts is ideal in the following scenarios:

- You want to generate income from premiums.

- You are willing to buy the stock at the strike price if necessary.

- You have sufficient cash to cover the potential purchase.

Wrapping Up

Beginner-friendly strategies like covered calls, protective puts, and selling cash-secured puts provide a solid foundation for entering the world of options trading. These low-risk approaches allow you to generate income, protect your investments, and acquire stocks at favorable prices. By mastering these strategies, you can build confidence and develop the skills needed to explore more advanced options trading techniques. As you gain experience, continue to refine your approach and adapt to changing market conditions, ensuring long-term success in your trading journey.

Chapter 5: Weekly Options for Beginners

Weekly options, often called "weeklies," have become popular in options trading. Their unique characteristics make them appealing to both beginner and experienced traders. Unlike traditional options contracts, which typically expire every month, weekly options offer more frequent expiration dates, providing traders with enhanced flexibility and opportunities to generate profits. In this chapter, we will explore the basics of weekly options, explain why they can be a valuable addition to your trading toolbox, discuss strategies for maximizing weekly gains, and identify common pitfalls to avoid.

Weekly Options Simplified

Weekly options function similarly to traditional contracts, with one primary distinction: they have a much shorter lifespan. Whereas standard options often have expirations that range from several weeks to several months (or even years for LEAPS), weekly options typically expire within five trading days. This shorter duration means they require a different trading and risk management approach.

What Are Weekly Options?

Weekly options are contracts introduced on Thursdays and expire the following Friday. Like standard options, weekly options give traders the right, but not the obligation, to buy or sell an underlying asset at a specified strike price before the expiration date. These options are available for underlying assets, including stocks, ETFs, and indices.

Key characteristics of weekly options include:

• **Short Expiration Period:** Weekly options have expiration dates that align with the end of the trading week, making them ideal for traders seeking short-term opportunities.

• **Lower Premiums:** Due to their shorter lifespan, weekly options generally have lower premiums than their monthly counterparts. This makes them more accessible for traders with smaller accounts.

• **Higher Sensitivity to Time Decay:** Weekly options experience accelerated time decay (theta) because they have less time until expiration. This characteristic can be advantageous for options sellers.

• **Frequent Opportunities:** The availability of new weekly options every week allows traders to capitalize on recurring opportunities in the market.

Why Weekly Options Are Unique

The primary appeal of weekly options lies in their flexibility and responsiveness to short-term market events. Unlike standard monthly options, which may tie up your capital for weeks, weekly options allow you to focus on specific, time-sensitive opportunities. They're ideal for capturing short-term trends or market volatility that arises from earnings announcements, geopolitical developments, or economic data releases.

For example, imagine a company set to release its quarterly earnings report on Wednesday. A trader could purchase a weekly call option expiring that Friday to profit from the stock's potential surge after the earnings beat expectations. Similarly, a bearish trader could buy a weekly put option to capitalize on a disappointing earnings report.

Why Trade Weekly Options?

Weekly options provide several benefits that make them attractive to both beginners and seasoned traders. Understanding these advantages can help you determine whether they align with your trading goals and risk tolerance.

1. Increased Flexibility

The frequent expiration dates of weekly options allow traders to adapt their strategies to changing market conditions. For example, suppose you anticipate a significant earnings announcement or economic report within the next few days. In that case, you can use weekly options to take advantage of the expected volatility without committing to a longer-term position.

2. Lower Capital Requirements

Because weekly options have lower premiums compared to standard options, they require less capital to trade. This makes them an ideal choice for beginners who may not have large accounts. Lower premiums also allow traders to execute multiple trades within a week, increasing the potential for diversification.

3. Enhanced Profit Potential

The short duration of weekly options creates opportunities for quick gains. Suppose the underlying asset experiences a significant price movement within the five-day timeframe. In that case, traders can achieve substantial returns relatively quickly. For instance, if a stock surges 10% due to a favorable announcement, weekly call options could yield several hundred percent returns.

4. Opportunities for Income Generation

For options sellers, weekly options provide an excellent way to generate consistent income. The accelerated time decay of weekly options works in their favor, as the value of the alternatives diminishes rapidly as expiration approaches. Selling strategies such as covered calls or cash-secured puts can be particularly effective when applied to weekly options.

5. Hedging Short-Term Risks

Weekly options can also be a hedging tool to protect your portfolio from short-term market fluctuations. For example, if you hold a long position in a stock and are concerned about potential downside risk over the next few days, purchasing a weekly put option can provide temporary protection.

6. Event-Specific Trading Opportunities

Weekly options benefit trading around specific events, such as earnings announcements, economic data releases, or Federal

Reserve meetings. These events often create short-term volatility, and weekly options allow traders to capitalize on these price movements without committing to longer-term contracts.

7. Leveraging Technical Analysis

For traders who rely on technical analysis, weekly options provide the perfect timeframe to act on short-term patterns, such as breakouts, reversals, or consolidation phases. By aligning the expiration date with the expected duration of the pattern, traders can optimize their profits.

Strategies to Maximize Weekly Gains

Trading weekly options requires a well-thought-out approach to maximize profits while managing risk. Below are several strategies that can help you capitalize on the unique characteristics of weekly options.

1. The Quick Profit Strategy

Weekly options are susceptible to price movements in the underlying asset. This makes them ideal for traders looking to profit from short-term price swings. To execute this strategy:

• Identify stocks or ETFs likely to experience significant price movement within the week. This could be due to earnings announcements, economic data releases, or technical patterns.

• Use at-the-money (ATM) or slightly out-of-the-money (OTM) options to maximize leverage.

• Set a clear exit plan, such as taking profits when the option premium increases by a certain percentage or cutting losses if the trade moves against you.

2. Selling Options for Time Decay

The accelerated time decay of weekly options can be advantageous for sellers. Strategies like selling covered calls or cash-secured puts can help you generate consistent income:

• Covered Calls: If you own at least 100 shares of a stock, you can sell a weekly call option against your position. This allows you to collect the Premium while maintaining ownership of your shares.

• Cash-Secured Puts: If you're willing to buy a stock at a lower price, you can sell a weekly put option and set aside enough cash to purchase the stock if assigned.

These strategies work best in low-volatility environments, where the underlying asset is unlikely to experience significant price swings.

3. Iron Condors for Range-Bound Markets

Iron condors are a popular strategy for weekly options when you expect the underlying asset to remain within a specific price range:

• Sell an OTM call and an OTM put.

• Buy a further OTM call and to limit potential losses.

- Collect the net Premium from the trade and profit if the asset stays within the defined range at expiration.

Iron condors are particularly effective when trading indices or ETFs, as these assets exhibit less volatility than individual stocks.

4. Straddles and Strangles for High Volatility

If you anticipate significant price movement but are unsure of the direction, straddles and strangles can be effective:

- Straddles: Buy a call and a put option with the same strike price and expiration date. This strategy profits from large price swings in either direction.

- Strangles: Buy an OTM call and an OTM put with the same expiration date. This approach is cheaper than a straddle but requires a more significant price movement to be profitable.

These strategies are best used when the market is about to experience a significant event, such as an earnings announcement or Federal Reserve decision.

5. Scalping Weekly Options

Scalping involves taking advantage of small price movements in the underlying asset or the options premium. Weekly options are ideal for scalping because prices can change rapidly due to high sensitivity to underlying price movements and time decay.

- Use technical indicators such as moving averages or RSI to identify entry and exit points.

- Focus on highly liquid options to minimize the bid-ask spread.

- Keep trades short to capitalize on quick price changes without being exposed to excessive risk.

Avoiding Common Pitfalls

While weekly options offer exciting opportunities, they also come with unique challenges. These pitfalls can help you avoid costly mistakes and improve your trading performance.

1. Overtrading

The frequent availability of weekly options can tempt traders to overtrade, leading to excessive transaction costs and emotional decision-making. To avoid this:

- Develop a trading plan with precise entry and exit criteria.

- Limit the number of trades you execute weekly to focus on high-probability opportunities.

2. Ignoring Time Decay

Time decay is more pronounced in weekly options, which can work against you if you're buying options. To mitigate this risk:

- Avoid holding long positions in weekly options until the last day of expiration unless the underlying asset moves in your favor.

- Consider selling options to take advantage of time decay instead of buying them.

Wrapping Up

Weekly options are a powerful trading tool that offers unique advantages, such as flexibility, low capital requirements, and enhanced profit potential. By understanding how to leverage these advantages while avoiding common pitfalls, you can add weekly options to your trading arsenal confidently and effectively.

Chapter 6: Reading the Options Chain

The options chain is one of the most essential tools in options trading. It serves as a map to help you identify opportunities, evaluate risks, and execute strategies effectively. Learning to read and analyze an options chain is a key step for beginners in developing trading confidence and proficiency. This chapter will demystify the options chain by exploring how to spot opportunities in strike prices, simplify expiration cycles, and identify liquid options to ensure smoother trading.

The Options Chain: An Overview

An options chain is a detailed table or list that displays all available options contracts for a specific underlying asset. Each contract listed provides critical data such as expiration dates, strike prices, bid and ask prices, implied volatility, and open interest. Traders use this information to evaluate profitability and risks when trading specific options.

Components of an Options Chain

The options chain is divided into two main sections: call options on one side and put options on the other. Below is an explanation of its key elements:

1.   **Underlying Asset Price:** The current market price of the traded stock or ETF. For reference, this price is often displayed at the top or center of the options chain.

2.   **Strike Prices:** These are the prices at which the underlying asset can be bought (for calls) or sold (for puts). Strike prices are listed in increments (e.g., $1, $2.50, or $5), representing key decision points for traders.

3.   **Expiration Dates:** The dates on which options contracts expire. Traders can choose from weekly, monthly, or even longer-term expiration dates.

4.   **Bid Price** is the highest price a buyer is willing to pay for an options contract.

5.   The ask **Price** is the lowest price a seller is willing to accept for an options contract.

6.   **Implied Volatility (IV):** A measure of the market's expectations for future price fluctuations of the underlying asset. A higher IV suggests a more significant potential movement in the asset's price.

7.   **Open Interest:** The total number of outstanding options contracts for a particular strike price and expiration date.

Each component plays a critical role in evaluating a trade's potential profitability and risks.

Why the Options Chain Matters

For traders, the options chain provides actionable insights into market sentiment, liquidity, and pricing dynamics. For example:

•   High open interest and trading volume at specific strike prices indicate strong market sentiment or expectations for significant movement in the underlying asset.

- Comparing bid and ask prices reveals liquidity, allowing traders to minimize transaction costs.

- Implied volatility helps traders anticipate the magnitude of potential price swings, guiding them in selecting appropriate strategies.

The options chain is more than a collection of numbers—it's a treasure trove of information that can help you align your trades with your financial goals.

Spotting Opportunities in Strike Prices

The strike price is one of the most critical factors when evaluating an options trade. It represents the price at which the option can be exercised, and its selection significantly affects potential profits, losses, and overall risk exposure.

What to Look for in Strike Prices?

1. At-the-Money (ATM) Strike Prices: ATM options are the most closely aligned with the current market price of the underlying asset. These options tend to have the highest extrinsic value (time value). They are often favored by traders seeking a balance between risk and reward.

2. In-the-Money (ITM) Strike Prices: ITM options have strike prices below the market price for calls and above the market price for puts. These options have intrinsic value and are considered safer but more expensive. They are suitable for traders looking for a higher probability of profit.

3.　　Out-of-the-Money (OTM) Strike Prices: OTM options have strike prices above the market price for calls and below the market price for puts. These options are cheaper but riskier, as they have no intrinsic value. They are commonly used in speculative trades with high potential returns.

Factors to Consider When Choosing Strike Prices

• 　　**Your Trading Objective:** Your choice of strike price should align with your trading goals. For instance, speculative trades may favor OTM options, while conservative strategies may require ITM options.

• 　　**Risk Tolerance:** Consider how much risk you are willing to take. ITM options are at lower risk, while OTM options are at higher risk but offer greater potential returns.

• 　　**Market Volatility:** If implied volatility is high, there's a greater chance for significant price movements. In such cases, traders might lean toward OTM options to capture more substantial price swings.

• 　　**Time to Expiration:** Options with more time to expiration give the underlying asset more opportunity to reach the strike price, which can influence your choice.

Advanced Considerations for Strike Prices

1.　　Delta Impact: Delta, one of the Greeks, measures the likelihood of an option expiring in the money. Options with a delta between 0.5 and 0.7 are often suitable for beginners because they effectively balance risk and reward.

2. Market Catalysts: Keep an eye on earnings announcements, product launches, or macroeconomic events that could push the underlying asset significantly in one direction. These catalysts may help you choose strike prices likely to benefit from the movement.

Example of Choosing Strike Prices

Let's say a stock is trading at $100:

• **ITM Option:** A call option with a strike price of $95 has intrinsic value and costs $6. This is a safer choice with a higher probability of profit.

• **ATM Option:** A call option with a strike price of $100 costs $3.50. It offers a balanced risk-reward profile.

• **OTM Option:** A call option with a strike price of $105 costs $1.50. If the stock price surges, it's a speculative play with high potential returns.

Analyzing these strike prices lets you select the option that best matches your market outlook and strategy.

Expiration Cycles Made Easy

Understanding expiration cycles is crucial for timing your trades effectively and managing risks. Options contracts have various expiration dates, from weekly to monthly, and even longer-term durations.

Types of Expiration Cycles

1.   Weekly Options: Weekly options expire every Friday, except when holidays affect the trading calendar. These contracts are ideal for short-term trades based on specific market events.

2.   Monthly Options: The most widely traded options expire on the third Friday of each month. They offer more time for market trends to develop and are suitable for medium-term strategies.

3.   LEAPS (Long-Term Equity Anticipation Securities): LEAPS are options with expiration dates extending a year or more into the future. They are often used for long-term speculation or portfolio hedging.

Choosing the Right Expiration Date

Your choice of expiration date should align with your trading strategy:

•   Short-Term Strategies: Weekly options work well for trades based on earnings announcements or other short-term catalysts.

•   Medium-Term Strategies: Monthly options balance time value and cost, making them ideal for trend-following strategies.

•   Long-Term Strategies: LEAPS are best for investors with a long-term outlook or those hedging against market risks.

Time Decay and Expiration Cycles

Time decay (theta) is a key consideration when selecting an expiration date. Options lose value as they approach expiration, with the rate of decay-accelerating in the final weeks. For buyers, choosing longer expirations can reduce the impact of time decay. At the same time, sellers benefit from the rapid decay of short-term options.

Example of Timing Expiration Cycles

Imagine you're trading a stock that is expected to announce its earnings in two weeks:

• A weekly option expiring this Friday might not capture the price movement resulting from the announcement, making it less effective.

• A monthly option expiring in four weeks provides sufficient time for the stock to react to the earnings report.

• A LEAPS option would be unnecessary for a short-term event, as it carries additional time value that may not align with your goals.

Aligning the expiration date with your trading strategy can maximize the profitability of your trades.

How to Identify Liquid Options?

Liquidity is essential in options trading, impacting your ability to enter and exit trades efficiently. Illiquid options can lead to wider bid-ask spreads, higher transaction costs, and difficulty executing trades.

What Makes an Option Liquid?

1.   High Open Interest: Open interest measures the number of outstanding contracts for a specific strike price and expiration date. Higher open interest indicates active market participation, translating to more effortless trade execution.

2.   High Trading Volume: Trading volume reflects the number of contracts traded within a period. Higher volume is a strong indicator of liquidity.

3.   Narrow Bid-Ask Spreads: The difference between the bid and ask prices should be minimal. Narrow spreads indicate a more efficient market with active buyers and sellers.

4.   Popular Underlying Assets: Options on highly traded stocks, ETFs, and indices tend to have better liquidity than those on less popular assets.

How to Assess Liquidity

Before entering a trade, evaluate the liquidity of the options contract:

•   Check the open interest and trading volume for the specific strike price and expiration date.

•   Compare the bid-ask spread. A spread of $0.05 or less is considered highly liquid, while a spread of $0.20 or more may indicate low liquidity.

•   Stick to options on popular stocks or ETFs with consistent trading activity.

Example of Identifying Liquid Options

Suppose you're considering two call options for a stock trading at $100:

- Option A:
- Strike Price: $105
- Open Interest: 10,000
- Bid-Ask Spread: $0.05
- Option B:
- Strike Price: $110
- Open Interest: 500
- Bid-Ask Spread: $0.30

Option A is significantly more liquid, making it a better choice for efficient trading. Option B, with low open interest and widespread, could be more challenging to trade profitably.

Wrapping Up

Mastering the options chain is a foundational skill for successful options trading. By learning to spot opportunities in strike prices, effectively time expiration cycles, and identify liquid options, you'll gain the confidence to make informed trading decisions. Over time, the options chain will become second nature, a powerful tool to guide your trades and optimize your strategies.

Chapter 7: Mastering the Trading Mindset

In the trading world, mastering the technical and analytical aspects is only half the battle. The other half—arguably the more critical—is mastering your mindset. Trading psychology is the often-overlooked cornerstone of success in financial markets. This chapter delves into the psychological challenges traders face, offering actionable strategies for overcoming fear and greed, staying disciplined in volatile markets, and building unshakable confidence.

Trading Psychology for Beginners

When you first enter the trading world, it's easy to focus on charts, indicators, and strategies while overlooking the emotional rollercoaster accompanying financial decision-making. However, seasoned traders often emphasize that your mindset can decide between consistent profits and devastating losses.

Trading psychology refers to the mental and emotional aspects that influence decision-making. It encompasses how you handle stress, uncertainty, and the inevitable ups and downs of the market. Without a solid psychological foundation, even the best trading strategy can falter.

For beginners, it's crucial to recognize that trading is not a get-rich-quick scheme. Unrealistic expectations often lead to frustration, impulsive decisions, and eventual burnout. Instead, approach trading with a mindset of gradual improvement and long-term growth. Understand that losses are part of the process, and your goal should be to manage risk while letting your edge play out over time.

A practical tip for beginners is to start small. Use a demo account or trade with minimal capital to gain experience without the pressure of significant financial risk. During this phase, pay attention to your emotions. Do you feel anxious before placing a trade? Do you panic when the market moves against you? Identifying these emotional triggers early on will help you develop strategies to manage them.

Another essential concept for beginners is the importance of patience. Markets often move in cycles, and not every moment is ideal for trading. Waiting for the proper setup can be challenging but crucial for long-term success. Impatience usually leads to overtrading, which increases transaction costs and emotional fatigue. Instead, focus on quality over quantity, and remember that sometimes the best trade is no trade at all.

Overcoming Fear and Greed

Fear and greed are the primary emotions derailing even the most well-thought-out trading plans. Fear can paralyze you, causing you to miss opportunities, while greed can lead to overtrading and excessive risk-taking.

Fear: The Silent Saboteur

Fear manifests in various ways, such as hesitating to enter a trade, closing a position too early, or avoiding the market altogether after a string of losses. This emotion is rooted in the fear of failure and the pain of losing money. While fear is a natural response, it becomes detrimental when it prevents you from executing your trading plan.

The key to overcoming fear is preparation. A solid trading plan backed by thorough analysis makes you less likely to second-guess yourself. Setting stop-loss orders can also alleviate the fear of catastrophic losses, as they define your maximum risk for each trade.

Mindfulness practices, such as meditation and deep breathing exercises, can help you stay calm and focused during stressful market conditions. Training yourself to stay present can reduce the emotional impact of past losses or future uncertainties.

Visualization techniques can also be influential in overcoming fear. Before entering a trade, visualize the entire process, including how you'll handle potential losses. This mental rehearsal can make the experience feel more familiar and less intimidating, reducing fear's hold on you.

Greed: The Temptation to Overreach

When a trade goes well, greed often shows up, and you're tempted to let it ride far beyond your original target. It can also manifest as chasing trades, increasing your position size recklessly, or ignoring your risk management rules in pursuit of higher profits.

To counteract greed, establish clear profit targets and stick to them. Understand that no single trade will make or break your trading career. Consistency is far more critical than hitting home runs. Keeping a trading journal can also help you identify patterns of greed-driven behavior, enabling you to address them proactively.

Finally, adopt a mindset of gratitude and contentment. Celebrate small wins and recognize that every profitable trade is a step toward your long-term goals, no matter how modest. When you focus on the process rather than the outcome, greed loses its grip on your decision-making.

A valuable strategy to combat greed is the "trade-and-walk" approach. Step away from the market once you hit your daily or weekly profit target. This prevents you from overtrading and reinforces the habit of disciplined decision-making.

Staying Disciplined in Volatile Markets

Volatility is both a blessing and a curse for traders. While it creates opportunities for significant profits, it also amplifies the emotional challenges of trading. Staying disciplined during turbulent market conditions requires preparation, self-control, and adaptability.

Develop a Robust Trading Plan

Options Trading for Beginners

Your trading plan is your roadmap for navigating the markets. It should outline your entry and exit criteria, risk management rules, and strategies for different market conditions. A clear plan reduces the likelihood of impulsive decisions, as you'll have a predefined course of action.

Before entering a trade, ask yourself:

- Does this trade align with my strategy?
- What is my risk-to-reward ratio?
- Where will I set my stop-loss and take-profit levels?

Answering these questions ensures that every trade is purposeful and aligned with your goals.

Embrace Routine and Consistency

Discipline thrives on routine. Set specific trading hours and stick to them, even if the market is open 24/7. Regularly review your trading plan and journal to reinforce good habits and identify areas for improvement.

Consistency also applies to risk management. Avoid drastically increasing your position size after a winning streak or chasing losses by doubling down. Stick to your predetermined risk parameters, typically risking no more than 1-2% of your trading capital on a single trade.

Manage Emotional Triggers

87

Volatile markets can evoke strong emotional reactions, from euphoria during a rally to despair during a sell-off. Recognizing these triggers is the first step to managing them effectively.

For example, if you panic during sharp price swings, practice stepping away from your trading screen. A brief pause can help you regain perspective and prevent rash decisions. Additionally, remind yourself that volatility is a natural part of the market and often creates the best trading opportunities when approached with a clear head.

Use Technology to Your Advantage

Modern trading platforms offer tools like automated alerts, trailing stop-loss orders, and algorithmic trading strategies. Leveraging these tools can help you stay disciplined by removing some of the emotional aspects of trading. For instance, a trailing stop-loss automatically adjusts as the market moves in your favor, locking in profits without requiring constant monitoring.

Adapt to Changing Market Conditions

Flexibility is a key component of discipline. Markets are dynamic, and what works in one scenario may not work in another. Stay open to refining your strategies based on market feedback, but ensure that any changes are deliberate and well-tested rather than reactive.

Building Confidence as a Trader

Confidence is a byproduct of preparation, experience, and self-belief. While it's normal to feel uncertain as a beginner, building confidence over time is essential for long-term success.

Start Small and Build Gradually

Confidence grows with experience, and experience doesn't require taking massive risks. Begin with small position sizes and gradually increase them as you become more comfortable with your strategy and the market dynamics. This approach minimizes the emotional impact of losses and allows you to focus on honing your skills.

Learn from Every Trade

Whether a trade results in a profit or a loss, there's always a lesson to be learned. Use your trading journal to document your thought process, emotions, and outcomes for each trade. Over time, you'll identify patterns and areas for improvement, boosting your confidence in your ability to adapt and grow.

Celebrate Progress, Not Perfection

Trading is a journey, not a destination. Instead of striving for perfection, aim for consistent improvement. Celebrate milestones such as achieving a positive monthly return, sticking to your trading plan, or overcoming a psychological hurdle. These small victories reinforce your confidence and keep you motivated.

Surround Yourself with Supportive Influences

The trading community can be a valuable source of encouragement and knowledge. Join forums, attend webinars, or connect with other traders who share your goals. Sharing experiences and learning from others can boost your confidence and provide fresh perspectives on your challenges.

Visualize Success

Visualization is a powerful tool for building confidence. Spend a few minutes each day imagining yourself executing trades flawlessly, managing risk effectively, and achieving your financial goals. This mental rehearsal reinforces positive habits and helps you approach the market with a success-oriented mindset.

Focus on Long-Term Goals

Confidence grows when you align your daily actions with broader financial and personal goals. Keeping your eye on the bigger picture makes you less likely to be derailed by short-term setbacks or market noise. Please write down your goals and review them regularly to stay motivated and confident.

Conclusion

Mastering the trading mindset is a continuous process that evolves with your experience and growth as a trader. By addressing the psychological challenges of fear and greed, staying disciplined in volatile markets, and building confidence, you'll position yourself for long-term success.

Remember that trading is as much about managing yourself as it is about managing your trades. Embrace the journey, stay committed to your personal and professional development, and let your mindset become your greatest asset in the markets. You can achieve the psychological resilience needed to thrive as a trader with patience and persistence.

Chapter 8: Creating a Winning Trading Plan

A winning trading plan is the foundation of consistent market success. It serves as your roadmap, guiding your decisions and controlling your emotions. Without a clear strategy, even the most talented traders can succumb to impulsive actions, emotional trading, and inconsistent results. In this chapter, we will explore the components of a robust trading plan, the importance of setting realistic goals, the value of backtesting, and the necessity of adapting your strategy to ever-changing market conditions.

Setting Realistic Goals

The first step in creating a trading plan is to define your goals. These goals should be clear, measurable, and realistic. Many beginners set overly ambitious targets, such as doubling their monthly account balance or achieving a 100% win rate. While optimism is essential, unrealistic goals can lead to frustration, reckless behavior, and failure.

Short-Term vs. Long-Term Goals

It's helpful to break your goals into short-term and long-term categories. Short-term goals might include achieving an inevitable percentage return over the next month or improving your trading discipline by sticking to your plan. Long-term goals could involve reaching a specific account size, gaining enough experience to trade full-time, or diversifying into multiple asset classes.

For example:

• Short-Term Goal: Maintain a risk-to-reward ratio 1:2 on all trades for the next three months.

• Long-Term Goal: Achieve an average annual return of 15% over five years while minimizing drawdowns.

Process-Oriented vs. Outcome-Oriented Goals

Many traders focus solely on outcome-oriented goals, such as achieving a specific profit target. However, process-oriented goals are equally, if not more, important. These goals emphasize the behaviors and habits that lead to long-term success, such as following your trading plan, journaling every trade, and consistently managing risk.

By prioritizing the process, you can build a strong foundation for success regardless of short-term outcomes. Over time, this approach will naturally lead to improved performance and profitability.

Managing Expectations

It's crucial to manage your expectations as a trader. Markets are unpredictable, and even the most experienced traders face losing streaks. A realistic perspective can prevent you from overreacting to short-term setbacks and keep you focused on the bigger picture. Remember, consistency and discipline are more important than quick profits.

The Importance of Backtesting

Backtesting is the process of evaluating a trading strategy using historical market data. It allows you to see how your strategy would have performed in the past, providing valuable insights into its potential effectiveness. Backtesting is essential in building confidence in your trading plan and avoiding costly mistakes in live markets.

Why Backtesting Matters

1.   Validation of Strategy: Backtesting helps confirm whether your strategy has a statistical edge. If a strategy consistently produces positive results over a significant sample size, it's more likely to succeed in live markets.

2.   Identifying Weaknesses: Backtesting can reveal flaws in your strategy, such as poor performance during certain market conditions or excessive drawdowns. You can refine your approach before risking real money by identifying these weaknesses.

3.   Building Confidence: Knowing that your strategy has worked in the past can boost your confidence and reduce emotional decision-making during live trading.

4.   Improving Risk Management: Backtesting helps you understand the risk profile of your strategy, including maximum

drawdowns and win/loss ratios. This information is critical for setting appropriate position sizes and stop-loss levels.

How to Backtest Effectively

1.   Use Reliable Data: Ensure your historical data is accurate and covers various market conditions. This includes trending markets, sideways markets, and periods of high and low volatility.

2.   Simulate Realistic Conditions: Account for factors such as slippage, commissions, and spreads. Overlooking these elements can lead to overly optimistic results that don't reflect real-world performance.

3.   Test a Large Sample Size: The more trades you include in your backtest, the more reliable the results. A small sample size can lead to misleading conclusions due to randomness.

4.   Analyze Key Metrics: Focus on win rate, average risk-to-reward ratio, maximum drawdown, and overall profitability. These metrics provide a comprehensive view of your strategy's performance.

5.   Document Your Findings: Keep detailed records of your backtesting results, including charts and notes. This documentation will be invaluable when refining your strategy or explaining your approach to others.

Avoiding Backtesting Pitfalls

While backtesting is a powerful tool, it's not without its limitations. Overfitting is a common pitfall, where traders tweak their strategies to perform exceptionally well on historical data but fail in live markets. To avoid overfitting, keep your strategy simple and focus on robust principles likely to hold up across different market environments.

Another common mistake is neglecting forward testing. Forward testing involves applying your strategy in a simulated or live market environment to validate its performance under current conditions. Combining backtesting with forward testing provides a complete picture of your strategy's potential.

Adapting Your Plan to Market Changes

Financial markets are dynamic and constantly influenced by economic events, technological advancements, and shifts in investor sentiment. A trading plan that worked well in one market environment may struggle in another. Adapting your strategy to changing market conditions is essential for long-term success.

Recognizing Market Regimes

Market regimes refer to the prevailing conditions in the financial markets, such as trending, ranging, or volatile environments. Each regime presents unique challenges and opportunities, requiring different strategies and approaches.

For example:

• Trending Markets: Favor trend-following strategies such as moving average crossovers or breakout trades.

- Ranging Markets: Work well with mean-reversion strategies, such as trading support and resistance levels or oscillators like RSI.

- Volatile Markets: Require a focus on risk management and possibly shorter timeframes to capitalize on rapid price movements.

Recognizing the current market regime allows you to adjust your trading plan accordingly. This might involve switching to a different strategy, modifying risk parameters, or sitting on the sidelines until conditions improve.

Continuous Learning and Improvement

The best traders are lifelong learners who constantly seek to improve their skills and adapt to new challenges. Stay informed about market trends, economic developments, and technological innovations that could impact your trading plan. Review your performance regularly and look for ways to refine your approach.

Some strategies for continuous improvement include:

- **Journaling:** Document every trade, including your rationale, emotions, and outcomes. Over time, this will help you identify strengths, weaknesses, and areas for growth.

- **Education:** Invest in books, courses, and mentorships to deepen your understanding of trading and the markets.

- **Networking:** Connect with other traders to share insights, strategies, and experiences.

Balancing Consistency with Flexibility

While adaptability is crucial, it's equally important to maintain consistency in your overall approach. Frequent, drastic changes to your trading plan can lead to confusion and lack of focus. Instead, aim for a balanced approach that allows for incremental adjustments based on objective data and market feedback.

Leveraging Technology

Technology can play a pivotal role in helping you adapt to market changes. Use advanced trading platforms and tools to analyze market trends, test new strategies, and automate certain aspects of your trading. Algorithmic trading, for example, allows you to execute trades based on predefined criteria, reducing the emotional impact of decision-making.

Building Your Trading Plan Step by Step

Now that we've covered the key elements of a trading plan let's outline a step-by-step process for creating one:

1.   Define Your Goals: Clearly articulate your short-term and long-term objectives, focusing on outcomes and processes.
2.   Choose Your Markets: Decide which assets or markets you'll trade, such as stocks, forex, commodities, or cryptocurrencies. Specializing in a specific market can help you develop expertise and gain an edge.
3.   Select Your Strategy: Based on your analysis, risk tolerance, and market conditions, identify the trading strategies

you'll use. These might include trend-following, mean-reversion, or breakout strategies.

4.   Establish Risk Management Rules: Determine your position sizing, maximum risk per trade, and overall risk exposure. For example, you might decide to risk no more than 1% of your account balance on any single trade.

5.   Set Entry and Exit Criteria: Define the specific conditions that will trigger your trades, including entry signals, stop-loss levels, and profit targets. Be as detailed as possible to reduce ambiguity.

6.   Create a Routine: Develop a daily or weekly routine that includes market analysis, trade execution, and performance review. Consistency in your routine helps reinforce discipline and focus.

7.   Backtest and Forward Test: Validate your strategy using historical data (backtesting) and live market simulations (forward testing) to ensure effectiveness and robustness.

8.   Monitor and Adjust: Regularly review your performance and make data-driven adjustments to your plan as needed. Be open to learning and evolving while staying true to your core principles.

Conclusion

Creating a winning trading plan is a dynamic process that requires careful planning, continuous learning, and adaptability. By setting realistic goals, backtesting your strategies, and adjusting to market changes, you can build a solid foundation for long-term success. Remember that the best trading plans are not set in stone; they evolve as you gain experience and the markets change.

A well-crafted trading plan improves your performance and reduces stress and emotional decision-making. It provides clarity and structure, enabling you to approach the markets with confidence and discipline. Whether you're a beginner or an experienced trader, investing time and effort into your trading plan is one of the most valuable steps you can take on your journey to financial success.

Chapter 9: The Greeks Demystified

Understanding the Greeks is essential for anyone looking to trade options effectively. These metrics quantify the various risks associated with options and provide insights into how their prices change in response to market conditions. By mastering the Greeks—Delta, Gamma, Theta, and Vega—traders can manage risk more effectively, make informed decisions, and apply strategies that align with their objectives. This chapter will explain these concepts in depth, illustrate how to use them to manage risk and explore practical applications for everyday trading.

Delta: Measuring Price Sensitivity

Delta represents an option's price sensitivity to changes in the underlying asset's price. In simpler terms, Delta indicates how much the cost of an option is expected to move for every $1 change in the underlying asset.

Key Points About Delta:

• **Call Options:** Delta values for call options range from 0 to +1. A Delta of 0.5 means the option price will move $0.50 for every $1 move in the underlying asset.

• **Put Options:** Delta values for put options range from 0 to -1. A Delta of -0.4 means the option price will move—$0.40 for every $1 move in the underlying asset.

- **Delta as Probability:** Delta is often used to estimate the probability that an option will expire in the money. For example, a Delta of 0.7 suggests a 70% chance the option will finish in the money.

Using Delta:

- Hedging: Delta helps traders hedge their positions by calculating the options needed to offset risk in the underlying asset. For instance, owning 100 shares of a stock can be offset by selling call options with a Delta of 0.5.

- Directional Strategies: Traders use Delta to assess how their portfolio will react to price changes, enabling them to adjust positions for desired exposure.

- Delta Neutral Strategies: Advanced traders often use Delta-neutral portfolios, where the combined Delta of all positions equals zero. This allows them to profit from time decay or volatility changes while minimizing directional risk.

Gamma: The Rate of Delta Change

Gamma measures how much Delta changes in response to a $1 move in the underlying asset. While Delta tells you how an option's price reacts to price changes, Gamma indicates how stable or unstable that relationship is.

Key Points About Gamma:

- **High Gamma:** Options close to being at the money have the highest Gamma values. Their Delta can change rapidly as the underlying asset's price moves.

- **Low Gamma:** Deep-in-the-money or far-out-of-the-money options have low Gamma, indicating more minor changes in Delta.

- **Impact on Hedging:** When Gamma is high, traders must adjust their hedges more frequently because Delta changes quickly.

Using Gamma:

- Hedging Adjustments: Gamma helps traders maintain a consistent Delta hedge by showing how much Delta will shift with price movements.

- Volatility Management: High Gamma can lead to significant gains or losses in volatile markets, so understanding Gamma can help traders manage risk effectively.

- Gamma Scalping: Gamma scalping is an advanced technique where traders dynamically hedge their positions to profit from small market movements. This strategy requires a deep understanding of both Gamma and Delta.

Theta: The Time Decay Factor

Theta measures how much an option's price decreases as time passes, assuming all other factors remain constant. Known as time decay, this is a critical factor for options traders.

Key Points About Theta:

• **Negative Theta:** Options lose value over time, so Theta is usually a negative number. For example, a Theta of -0.05 means the option loses $0.05 in value per day.

• **Effect on Short-Term Options:** Theta accelerates as expiration approaches, especially for at-the-money options.

• **Impact on Strategies:** Theta negatively affects long option positions (calls and puts), while time decay benefits short positions.

Using Theta:

• **Income Strategies:** Traders who sell options, such as in covered call or credit spread strategies, rely on Theta to generate profits from time decay.

• **Managing Risk:** Traders with long option positions must account for Theta's impact on their portfolio, particularly when holding options close to expiration.

Advanced Considerations for Theta:

• Weekly Options: Options with shorter expiration periods experience accelerated Theta decay. Traders focused on short-term strategies often capitalize on this rapid decay to maximize profits.

• Non-Linear Time Decay: Theta decay is not linear. It accelerates as expiration nears, requiring traders to adjust their strategies to manage the increasing impact of time decay.

• Theta and Volatility: While Theta generally erodes option value, spikes in volatility can offset time decay temporarily. Understanding this relationship is critical for balancing time-sensitive strategies.

Vega: Sensitivity to Volatility

Vega measures how much an option's price changes in response to a 1% change in implied volatility. Since volatility is a key driver of option prices, Vega is crucial for understanding potential price swings.

Key Points About Vega:

• Volatility Impact: High Vega means the option's price is susceptible to changes in implied volatility. For example, a Vega of 0.10 means the option's price will increase by $0.10 for every 1% increase in implied volatility.

• At-the-Money Options: Vega is highest for at-the-money options and decreases for deep-in-the-money or out-of-the-money options.

• Expiration Effect: Vega decreases as expiration approaches because changes in implied volatility have less impact on short-term options.

Using Vega:

• Volatility Trades: Traders can use Vega to capitalize on anticipated changes in volatility. For instance, buying options before earnings announcements (when volatility spikes) can be profitable.

• Risk Management: Understanding Vega helps traders manage the risk of sudden volatility changes, which can significantly impact option prices.

Strategies to Leverage Vega:

• Long Vega Strategies: Buying options or using long straddles can profit from expected increases in implied volatility.

• Short Vega Strategies: Selling options or credit spreads can benefit from stable or decreasing implied volatility, particularly in low-volatility environments.

• Vega Neutral Portfolios: Advanced traders can create portfolios with minimal Vega exposure, reducing the impact of volatility swings on overall performance.

How to Use Greeks to Manage Risk?

The Greeks are theoretical concepts and practical tools that help traders manage risk and optimize their strategies. Here's how you can use them effectively:

Delta for Directional Risk

• Portfolio Exposure: Use Delta to measure your portfolio's overall directional exposure. For example, a portfolio with a total Delta of +200 behaves like owning 200 shares of the underlying asset.

• Neutralizing Risk: Delta-neutral strategies, such as straddles and strangles, aim to minimize directional risk while profiting from other factors like volatility.

Gamma for Adjusting Positions

• Stability Management: High Gamma means your Delta can change rapidly, so monitor it closely in volatile markets to avoid overexposure.

• Scalping Opportunities: Gamma scalping involves minor position adjustments to capitalize on frequent Delta changes, which can be profitable in certain market conditions.

Theta for Time Decay

• Maximizing Profits: Short-term strategies, like selling covered calls, benefit from Theta as time decay accelerates.

• Avoiding Losses: Long-term option holders must monitor Theta closely, especially as expiration nears, to prevent significant value erosion.

Vega for Volatility Risk

• Hedging Volatility: If you expect a drop in implied volatility, consider selling options to benefit from decreasing Vega.

• Earnings Strategies: Use Vega to position yourself for volatility spikes around events like earnings announcements or economic data releases.

Combining Greeks for Holistic Risk Management:

- Multi-Dimensional View: Analyze all the Greeks for a complete picture of an option's risk profile. For instance, combining Delta and Vega can help you understand directional and volatility risks.

- Dynamic Adjustments: As market conditions change, use the Greeks to adjust your positions dynamically, ensuring alignment with your risk tolerance and market outlook.

Practical Applications of the Greeks

Understanding the Greeks allows traders to design and execute strategies tailored to their goals and market conditions. Here are some practical applications:

Income Generation

- Covered Calls: Selling call options against stock holdings generates income from Theta (time decay). Use Delta to select strike prices that balance risk and reward.

- Credit Spreads: Combining short and long options creates strategies like iron condors, which profit from time decay and stable markets. Vega and Theta play significant roles in these setups.

Hedging Strategies

- Protective Puts: Buying put options protects against downside risk in a stock portfolio. Delta and Vega help determine the cost and effectiveness of this hedge.

- Collars: A collar strategy combines a long stock position with a protective put and a short call. Greeks like Delta and Theta ensure the plan aligns with your risk tolerance.

Speculative Trades

- Directional Bets: Use Delta to select options with higher sensitivity to price changes for directional trades.

- • Volatility Plays: Long straddles or strangles can capitalize on movements in either direction when expecting significant volatility. Vega is critical for these trades.

Advanced Strategies

- Butterfly Spreads: These neutral strategies profit from low volatility and time decay. Theta is the primary driver of profits, while Vega indicates potential risks from volatility changes.

- Gamma Scalping: Active traders use Gamma to adjust positions dynamically, capturing profits from frequent price swings.

Real-Life Scenario:

- Imagine holding a portfolio of options before an earnings announcement. You can estimate how price changes, time decay, and volatility shifts will impact your positions by analyzing Delta, Theta, and Vega. This lets you adjust your trades anticipating the event, ensuring a well-balanced risk-reward profile.

Conclusion

The Greeks—Delta, Gamma, Theta, and Vega—are the building blocks of options trading. By understanding and applying these metrics, traders can manage risk effectively, optimize their strategies, and make informed decisions. While the concepts may seem complex initially, mastering the Greeks is essential for anyone serious about options trading.

Use Delta to measure directional exposure, Gamma to monitor stability, Theta to account for time decay, and Vega to navigate volatility. Together, these tools provide a comprehensive framework for analyzing and executing options strategies. With practice and experience, the Greeks will become second nature, empowering you to trade confidently and precisely.

Chapter 10: Advanced Options Strategies

Mastering advanced options strategies opens the door to more sophisticated ways to profit from the market while managing risk effectively. These strategies go beyond simple calls and address market conditions, such as low volatility, directional uncertainty, or time decay advantages. This chapter will explore Iron Condors, Butterflies, Straddles, Strangles, Calendar Spreads, and the art of rolling positions and making trade adjustments. Understanding how and when to use these strategies can enhance your trading repertoire and achieve more consistent results.

Iron Condors and Butterflies

Iron Condors and Butterfly spreads are advanced neutral strategies designed to capitalize on low-volatility markets. While they share similarities, their structures and risk/reward profiles differ significantly.

Iron Condors

An Iron Condor strategy involves selling an out-of-the-money put and call while simultaneously buying a further out-of-the-money put and call. The goal is to profit from a stable market where the underlying asset's price remains within a defined range.

How It Works:

1. **Sell a Put Option:** Strike price below the current market price.

2. **Sell a Call Option:** Strike price above the current market price.

3. **Buy a Protective Put:** Further out-of-the-money to limit downside risk.

4. **Buy a Protective Call:** Further out-of-the-money to limit upside risk.

Benefits:

- Limited risk and defined reward.

- Profits from low volatility.

- Flexible adjustment options.

Example:

Consider a stock trading at $100. You could sell a put with a $95 strike, sell a call with a $105 strike, buy a $90 protective put, and buy a $110 protective call. The maximum profit is achieved if the stock remains between $95 and $105 by expiration.

Advanced Applications:

- Use Iron Condors during earnings seasons for stocks that historically show minimal price movement post-announcement.

- Combine Iron Condors with other volatility strategies, such as Long Straddles, for a diversified portfolio.

Butterfly Spreads

A Butterfly Spread is another neutral strategy that involves using three-strike prices. It profits most when the underlying asset's price is near the middle strike at expiration. This strategy can be created using either calls or puts.

How It Works:

1. **Sell Two Options:** At the middle strike price.
2. **Buy One Option:** At a lower strike price.
3. **Buy One Option:** At a higher strike price.

Benefits:

• High potential reward relative to risk.

• Ideal for low-volatility markets.

• Defined risk and reward.

Example:

For a stock trading at $100, you could buy a $95 call, sell two $100 calls, and buy a $105 call. The maximum profit occurs if the stock closes at $100 at expiration.

Advanced Tips:

• Use Butterfly Spreads close to expiration to maximize the effects of time decay.

• Consider adjusting one leg if the market moves significantly to reduce potential losses.

• Apply directional Butterfly Spreads by skewing the strikes towards anticipated price movements.

Straddles, Strangles, and Calendar Spreads

Straddles, Strangles, and Calendar Spreads are strategies for traders anticipating specific market conditions, such as high volatility or time decay advantages.

Straddles

A Straddle involves buying a call and a put with the same strike price and expiration. This strategy profits from large price movements in either direction, making it ideal for volatile markets.

How It Works:

1. **Buy a Call Option:** At-the-money.
2. **Buy a Put Option:** At-the-money.

Benefits:

- Profits from large price movements in either direction.
- Simple to execute.

Example:

If a stock trades at $100, you could buy a $100 call and a $100 put. The strategy becomes profitable if the stock moves significantly above or below $100.

Risks and Considerations:

- Straddles can be expensive due to high premiums, particularly during elevated implied volatility.

- Use Straddles sparingly and only when you expect significant price movement.

Advanced Tips:

- Initiate Straddles before significant news events, such as earnings or product launches, to capture sharp price movements.
- Adjust one leg to convert the straddle into a directional trade if the price direction becomes apparent after the event.

Strangles

A Strangle is similar to a Straddle but uses out-of-the-money options. This reduces the upfront cost but requires a more significant price movement to achieve profitability.

How It Works:

1. **Buy a Call Option:** Out-of-the-money.
2. **Buy a Put Option:** Out-of-the-money.

Benefits:

- It's lower cost than a Straddle.
- Profits from large price movements.

Example:

For a stock trading at $100, you could buy a $105 call and a $95 put. The stock must move significantly above $105 or below $95 to make the strategy profitable.

Advanced Tips:

- Combine Strangles with event-based trading, such as earnings announcements or economic releases.

- Monitor implied volatility levels before entering a Strangle to avoid overpaying for options.

- Create an adjusted Strangle by adding a closer strike on one leg to capture smaller movements.

Calendar Spreads

A Calendar Spread involves selling a near-term option and buying a longer-term option with the same strike price. This strategy profits from time decay and differences in implied volatility.

How It Works:

1. **Sell a Short-Term Option:** At-the-money or slightly out-of-the-money.

2. **Buy a Long-Term Option:** Same strike price.

Benefits:

- Profits from time decay.

- It can be used in low-volatility markets.

- Limited risk.

Example:

If a stock is trading at $100, you could sell a $100 call expiring in one month and buy a $100 call expiring in three months. The strategy profits if the stock price remains near $100 as the short-term option expires.

Considerations:

• Calendar Spreads require careful monitoring of volatility changes.

• Use this strategy in markets with stable price action to maximize time decay advantages.

• Adjust the longer-term leg to capture evolving market trends if needed.

Rolling Positions and Trade Adjustments

Rolling positions and making trade adjustments are essential for managing risk and optimizing returns. These techniques allow traders to adapt to changing market conditions without closing their positions entirely.

Rolling Positions

Rolling involves closing an existing option position and simultaneously opening a new one with a different strike price, expiration, or both.

When to Roll:

• **To Extend Duration:** If you need more time for the trade to work in your favor.

• **To Adjust Strike Prices:** To reflect changes in market conditions or reduce risk.

- **To Lock in Profits:** Rolling to a less risky position while maintaining exposure.

Example:

If you sold a $100 call and the stock price rises to $105, you could roll the position by buying back the $100 call and selling a $110 call. This reduces your risk while still allowing for potential profit.

Advanced Rolling Strategies:

- Roll positions incrementally rather than making drastic changes to minimize transaction costs and slippage.
- Combine rolling with other adjustments, such as adding protective options, to balance the risk/reward profile.
- Roll-covered calls up and out to avoid losing shares while capturing additional premiums.

Trade Adjustments

Trade adjustments involve modifying an existing position to align with current market conditions. This can include adding options, changing strike prices, or adjusting expirations.

Common Adjustments:

1. **Adding Hedges:** To reduce risk, such as buying a protective put.
2. **Changing Strikes:** To capture more profit or reduce potential losses.

3. Converting Strategies: For example, turning a Straddle into an Iron Condor.

Benefits:

- Flexibility to respond to market changes.
- Improved risk management.
- Increased probability of success.

Example:

If you hold a Strangle and the underlying asset's price moves closer to one of the strikes, you could adjust the other leg to create a tighter range, converting it into a Butterfly Spread.

Tips for Effective Adjustments:

- Avoid over-adjusting, as this can lead to excessive transaction costs and complexity.
- Use adjustments as part of a well-defined trading plan rather than reacting emotionally to market movements.
- Monitor Greeks like Delta and Vega before making significant adjustments.

Practical Applications and Tips

Combining Strategies

Many traders combine strategies to achieve specific goals, such as income generation, directional speculation, or volatility plays. For example:

- Pair an Iron Condor with a Calendar Spread to profit from low volatility and time decay.
- Using a Straddle before earnings and rolling it into a Strangle after the event.

Risk Management

Advanced options strategies can be complex, so proper risk management is critical. Always:

- Define your maximum risk and reward before entering a trade.
- Monitor your positions closely.
- Be prepared to adjust or exit if the trade moves against you.

Choosing the Right Strategy

The best strategy depends on your market outlook, risk tolerance, and trading goals. Consider:

- **Market Conditions:** Use neutral strategies like Iron Condors in low-volatility markets and Straddles in high-volatility markets.
- **Time Horizon:** Short-term traders may prefer Calendar Spreads, while long-term traders might focus on Butterfly Spreads or rolling positions.

Conclusion

Advanced options strategies like Iron Condors, Butterflies, Straddles, Strangles, Calendar Spreads, and rolling positions offer traders powerful tools to navigate various market conditions. While these strategies require a deeper understanding of options and their risks, they can significantly enhance your ability to generate consistent returns and manage risk effectively.

By mastering these strategies and learning how to adjust positions dynamically, you can approach the markets with greater confidence and adaptability. Start small, practice diligently, and continuously refine your skills to achieve long-term success in options trading.

Advanced Insight: Leveraging Greeks in Advanced Strategies

To maximize the effectiveness of these advanced strategies, incorporate the Greeks into your analysis. For example:

• Delta: Use Delta to monitor directional exposure in Straddles and Strangles.

• Theta: Capitalize on time decay in Calendar Spreads and Iron Condors.

• Vega: Manage volatility risks effectively, particularly in event-driven trades like earnings.

By combining advanced strategies with a solid understanding of the Greeks, traders can build a more comprehensive and adaptive approach to options trading.

Chapter 11: Learning from Case Studies

Trading is a skill that requires both theoretical knowledge and practical experience. One of the best ways to learn is by analyzing real-world case studies, which reveal the pitfalls to avoid and the steps to emulate for success. This chapter will explore beginner mistakes and how to avoid them, walk through successful trade examples, and extract valuable insights from professional traders. By the end of this chapter, you will have a deeper understanding of what works and what doesn't and how to navigate the complexities of trading more confidently.

Beginner Mistakes and How to Avoid Them

Many traders start enthusiastically but lack the discipline and knowledge required to succeed. Here are some common mistakes beginners make and how to avoid them:

1. Lack of a Trading Plan

Many novice traders jump into the markets without a clear plan, relying on gut feelings or tips from others. This often leads to inconsistent results and emotional decision-making.

How to Avoid It:

• Create a detailed trading plan that outlines your goals, strategies, risk tolerance, and rules for entering and exiting trades.

• Please stick to your plan and review it regularly to make improvements.

2. Overleveraging

Leverage can amplify gains, but it also magnifies losses. Beginners often use excessive leverage, exposing themselves to unnecessary risks.

How to Avoid It:

• Use leverage sparingly, especially when you're just starting.

• Never risk more than 1-2% of your trading account on a single trade.

3. Ignoring Risk Management

Failing to set stop-loss orders or risking too much capital on a single trade can lead to significant losses.

How to Avoid It:

• Always set stop-loss and take-profit levels before entering a trade.

• Diversify your portfolio to spread risk.

4. Chasing the Market

Beginners often get caught up in market hype, buying at the top or selling at the bottom.

How to Avoid It:

• Avoid impulsive decisions. Analyze the market objectively and stick to your strategy.

- Use technical and fundamental analysis to identify good entry and exit points.

5. Emotional Trading

Fear and greed are two of the biggest obstacles for traders. Fear can cause you to exit trades too early, while greed can lead to holding positions too long.

How to Avoid It:

- Develop emotional discipline by following a structured trading plan.
- Take breaks and step away from the screen when emotions run high.

6. Overtrading

Many beginners believe that more trades mean more profits, but overtrading often leads to poor decision-making and increased transaction costs.

How to Avoid It:

- Focus on quality over quantity—only trade when a clear opportunity aligns with your strategy.
- Keep a trading journal to track your performance and identify patterns in your behavior.

7. Ignoring Market Conditions

Beginners sometimes fail to adjust their strategies based on changing market conditions, leading to avoidable losses.

How to Avoid It:

• Stay informed about macroeconomic events and market trends.

• Adjust your trading strategies for high volatility, low liquidity, or trending markets.

Successful Trade Examples Explained

Learning from successful trades can provide valuable insights into how to apply strategies effectively. Let's examine two case studies that highlight key principles of successful trading:

Case Study 1: Trend Following with a Moving Average Crossover

Background: A trader notices a stock trending upward over several weeks. They aim to capitalize on the trend using the moving average crossover strategy.

The Setup:

• The trader uses a 50-day moving average (MA) and a 200-day moving average.

• A buy signal is triggered when the 50-day MA exceeds the 200-day MA (golden cross).

The Execution:

- The trader buys 100 shares of the stock at $50 when the golden cross occurs.

- A stop-loss is set at $47 to limit downside risk.

- A take-profit target is set at $60 based on historical resistance levels.

The Outcome:

- The stock reaches $60 within three weeks, and the trader exits the position with a $1,000 profit.

Key Takeaways:

- The trader followed a proven strategy with precise entry and exit rules.

- The risk was managed effectively with a stop-loss order.

- Patience and discipline allowed the trade to reach its full potential.

Case Study 2: Earnings Volatility with an Options Straddle

Background: A trader anticipates high volatility in a stock ahead of its earnings report but is unsure of the direction.

The Setup:

- The stock is trading at $100.

- The trader buys a call option with a $100 strike price and a put option with a $100 strike price, both expiring in one week.

- The premium paid is $5 per option ($500 total).

The Execution:

- After the earnings report, the stock drops to $90 due to disappointing results.
- The put option gains significant value, while the call option expires worthless.

The Outcome:

- The trader sells the put option for $1,200, resulting in a net profit of $700 after accounting for the $500 cost.

Key Takeaways:

- The trader used a Straddle to profit from volatility without predicting the direction.
- Proper position sizing ensured the risk was manageable.
- Timing the trade around a known catalyst (earnings) increased the likelihood of success.

Case Study 3: Scalping in a High-Volatility Market

Background: During a volatile trading day, a professional scalper identifies opportunities to profit from rapid price movements.

The Setup:

- The trader monitors a stock with significant volume and a tight bid-ask spread.
- Using Level 2 data, they spot large buy and sell orders that indicate potential short-term price reversals.

The Execution:

- The trader buys 500 shares at $25.20 and immediately sets a limit sell order at $25.30.

- Within minutes, the stock price rises, and the order is executed.

The Outcome:

- The trader earns $50 in profit. Repeating this process multiple times daily generates cumulative gains of $500.

Key Takeaways:

- Scalping requires quick decision-making and precise execution.

- Monitoring liquidity and order flow is critical for success.

- Small, consistent profits can add up over time.

Insights from Professional Traders

Professional traders have years of experience and valuable lessons to share. Here are some key insights from successful traders that can help you elevate your trading game:

1. Focus on Risk Management

"Protecting your capital is more important than chasing profits." — Paul Tudor Jones

- Successful traders prioritize risk management above all else. They know that even the best strategies can fail without controlling risk.

- Always calculate your risk-to-reward ratio before entering a trade. Aim for a ratio of at least 1:2.

2. Master One Strategy Before Moving to Another

"You don't need to trade every strategy. Master one, and make it your own." — Linda Raschke

- Professional traders often specialize in one or two strategies they've mastered

- Before diversifying, perfect a single approach, such as trend following or mean reversion.

3. Adapt to Market Conditions

"The market is never wrong; your interpretation of it might be." — Jesse Livermore

- Markets are dynamic, and successful traders adapt their strategies to changing conditions.

- Regularly review your performance and adjust your approach based on what's working and what isn't.

4. Stay Disciplined

"Amateurs think about how much money they can make. Professionals think about how much money they could lose." — Jack Schwager

• Discipline separates successful traders from the rest. Following your plan and avoiding impulsive decisions is crucial.

• Use tools like alerts and automated orders to remove emotion from your trading.

5. Embrace Continuous Learning

"The more you learn, the more you earn." — Warren Buffett

• The best traders never stop learning. They read books, attend webinars, and stay updated on market trends.

• Keep a trading journal to document your successes and failures and learn from both.

• Think in Probabilities, Not Certainties

• "Trading is a game of probabilities, not certainties." — Mark Douglas

• Professional traders understand that no strategy has a 100% success rate. They focus on executing their plan consistently to achieve long-term profitability.

• Accept losses as part of the process and avoid overreacting to individual outcomes.

Applying Lessons from Case Studies

By studying real-world examples and learning from experienced traders, you can avoid common pitfalls and develop a more structured approach to trading. Here are some practical steps to apply these lessons:

1. Develop a Trading Plan:

- Use insights from successful trades to create a plan that suits your style and goals.
- Include clear rules for entry, exit, and risk management.

2. Practice with Paper Trading:

- Before risking real money, practice your strategies in a simulated environment.
- Analyze your performance and make adjustments as needed.

3. Stay Patient and Disciplined:

- Trading success doesn't happen overnight. Stay committed to your plan and focus on consistent execution.

4. Learn from Every Trade:

- Review winning and losing trades to identify what worked and what didn't.
- Keep a journal to track your progress and refine your approach over time.

5. Seek Mentorship:

- Learning from experienced traders can accelerate your growth.
- Join trading communities or invest in courses to gain valuable insights.

Conclusion

Case studies are a powerful tool for learning the art of trading. By analyzing beginner mistakes, successful trades, and professional insights, you can build a solid foundation for your trading journey. Remember that every trader's path is unique, and success comes from a combination of knowledge, discipline, and continuous improvement.

Use the lessons from this chapter to refine your strategies, manage risk effectively, and confidently approach the markets. You can turn trading into a rewarding and sustainable endeavor with practice and perseverance.

Additional Resources for Case Study Analysis

To further enhance your skills, consider using additional resources to analyze case studies and real-world scenarios:

1. **Trading Platforms with Replay Features:**
•   Some platforms allow you to replay historical price data and practice making decisions in real time.
2. **Books and Journals:**
•   Many professional traders share detailed case studies in their books. Look for titles by well-known authors like Jack Schwager or Mark Minervini.
3. **Online Communities:**

- Join forums or groups where traders discuss their trades and provide insights. Learning from others' experiences can be incredibly valuable.

These tools and resources will complement the lessons from this chapter and provide ongoing opportunities to refine your trading approach.

Chapter 12: Best Platforms and Tools for Beginners

Starting your trading journey can feel overwhelming, but the right platforms and tools can make all the difference. Whether managing trades, performing technical analysis, or seeking guidance from communities, this chapter will help you navigate the best resources available for beginners. We will explore free calculators and analysis tools that simplify trading decisions and discuss books, courses, and communities that foster continued learning.

Free Calculators and Analysis Tools

Having access to free tools can be a game-changer for beginners. These resources simplify complex calculations, enhance decision-making, and reduce the steep learning curve often associated with trading. Below are some essential tools to consider:

1. Position Size Calculators

Position sizing is crucial for effective risk management. A position size calculator helps determine the number of shares or contracts to trade based on your account size, risk tolerance, and stop-loss distance.

- **Example Tool:** MyFxBook's Position Size Calculator.
- **Benefits:** Prevents over-leveraging and ensures consistent risk management.

2. Profit and Loss (P&L) Calculators

Understanding potential profit or loss before entering a trade is vital. P&L calculators allow traders to analyze risk-to-reward ratios and evaluate whether a trade is worth taking.

- **Example Tool:** BabyPips' Profit Calculator.
- **Benefits:** It helps assess trade viability and align decisions with your trading plan.

3. Options Pricing Calculators

Options pricing can be complex due to the impact of variables like Delta, Theta, and implied volatility. Options pricing calculators make it easier to understand how these factors influence your trades.

- **Example Tool:** Options Profit Calculator.
- **Benefits:** Provides clarity on break-even points and profit potential for options trades.

4. Economic Calendars

An economic calendar displays key financial events, such as interest rate announcements, employment data, and GDP releases, which often drive market volatility.

- **Example Tool:** Investing.com's Economic Calendar.
- **Benefits:** Helps traders anticipate and prepare for market-moving events.

5. Charting Platforms

Visualizing price action and trends is essential for technical analysis. Free charting platforms provide tools for creating custom indicators, drawing trendlines, and setting alerts.

- **Example Tools**: TradingView (basic version) and StockCharts.
- **Benefits:** Enables detailed technical analysis with user-friendly interfaces.

6. Backtesting Tools

Backtesting allows traders to test strategies using historical data, providing insights into their performance before applying them in live markets.

- **Example Tool:** TradingView's strategy tester (basic features are free).
- **Benefits:** Increases confidence in your strategy by validating its effectiveness.

7. Volatility Trackers

Market volatility can significantly impact trading strategies. Volatility trackers monitor instruments like the VIX or implied volatility in options.

- **Example Tool:** CBOE's VIX Tracker.
- **Benefits:** Helps traders identify periods of high or low market uncertainty.

Books, Courses, and Communities for Continued Learning

Successful traders understand that learning is a lifelong journey. Below are some of the best resources to accelerate your growth as a trader:

Books

Books are timeless resources packed with knowledge from experienced traders. Here are some must-reads for beginners:

1.   "Trading for a Living" by Dr. Alexander Elder

• **Overview:** Covers psychology, technical analysis, and risk management in a comprehensive format.

• **Why It's Helpful:** Provides actionable strategies while emphasizing the importance of emotional discipline.

2.   "A Beginner's Guide to the Stock Market" by Matthew R. Kratter

• **Overview:** Simplifies the stock trading basics, making it perfect for beginners.

• **Why It's Helpful:** Offers clear, concise explanations without overwhelming jargon.

3.   "Technical Analysis of the Financial Markets" by John J. Murphy

- **Overview:** A foundational text on technical analysis, including chart patterns, indicators, and oscillators.

- **Why It's Helpful:** Equips traders with the tools for practical chart analysis.

4. **"Market Wizards" by Jack D. Schwager**

- **Overview:** A collection of interviews with some of the most successful traders in history.

- **Why It's Helpful:** Offers inspiration and practical advice from trading legends.

Courses

Online courses provide structured learning paths, often including video lessons, quizzes, and interactive content. Here are some top options:

1. **Investopedia Academy's Stock Market Courses**

- **Overview:** Covers the basics of trading, technical analysis, and portfolio management.

- **Cost:** Affordable, with beginner-friendly pricing.

- Why It's Helpful: Explicitly designed for those starting their trading journey.

2. **Babypips School of Pipsology**

- **Overview:** A free, in-depth guide to Forex trading.

- **Why It's Helpful:** Explains complex concepts in an easy-to-understand manner.

3. **Udemy's Trading and Technical Analysis Courses**

• **Overview:** Offers a wide range of affordable courses on stock trading, options, and technical analysis.

• **Why It's Helpful:** Provides lifetime access, allowing learners to revisit material as needed.

4. **Coursera: Financial Markets by Yale University**

• **Overview:** Taught by Nobel laureate Robert Shiller, this course explains how financial markets function.

• **Why It's Helpful:** Combines academic rigor with practical insights.

Communities

Being part of a community can provide support, accountability, and the opportunity to learn from others' experiences. Here are some recommended communities:

1. **Reddit (r/StockMarket, r/Options, r/DayTrading)**

• **Overview:** Subreddits where traders share ideas, strategies, and resources.

• **Why It's Helpful:** Free access to various perspectives and discussions.

2. **TradingView Social Community**

• **Overview:** A platform where traders publish and discuss chart ideas.

- **Why It's Helpful:** Encourages collaboration and learning from peers.

3. **Discord Trading Groups**

- **Overview:** Many trading communities have Discord servers for real-time discussions and alerts.

- **Why It's Helpful:** Enables instant communication and access to experienced traders.

4. **Professional Associations**

- **Examples:** Chartered Market Technician (CMT) Association.

- **Why It's Helpful:** Offers access to resources, networking opportunities, and certification programs.

Practical Tips for Using Platforms and Tools Effectively

1. **Start Small:**

- Use free or low-cost tools before investing in premium platforms.

- Focus on mastering one tool or platform at a time.

2. **Leverage Tutorials:**

- Many platforms offer tutorials and guides. Take the time to learn their features.

- YouTube is another excellent resource for platform walkthroughs.

3. Stay Organized:

- Please keep track of the tools you use and their specific purposes.

- Use spreadsheets or apps to document your trades, insights, and lessons learned.

4. Experiment and Adjust:

- Test different platforms to find the ones that best suit your trading style.

- Continuously evaluate whether your tools align with your evolving needs.

5. Engage with Communities:

- Ask questions, share insights, and participate actively in trading forums or groups.

- Learning from others' successes and mistakes can accelerate your growth.

Conclusion

As a beginner, the right platforms and tools can set the foundation for long-term success. From free calculators to advanced charting platforms, these resources simplify the trading process and help you make informed decisions. Additionally, investing in books, courses, and trading communities' fosters continued growth and builds the knowledge to navigate complex markets.

By combining these tools with consistent practice and a commitment to learning, you can confidently take your first steps toward becoming a successful trader. Remember, every expert was once a beginner—your journey starts here.

Chapter 13: Weekly Options in Practice

Weekly options, often called "weeklies," have gained immense popularity among traders due to their short expiration periods and high potential for quick profits. These options can be a powerful tool for maximizing gains but also present unique challenges. This chapter will explore combining strategies for maximum profitability and address traders' key challenges when dealing with weekly options.

Combining Strategies for Maximum Gains

Weekly options are versatile, allowing traders to employ various strategies depending on market conditions. By combining techniques, traders can optimize their risk-to-reward ratio and utilize weeklies' unique characteristics.

1. Using Iron Condors for Range-Bound Markets

Iron Condors are ideal for weekly options when the market is expected to remain within a specific range. This strategy involves selling a call spread and a put spread simultaneously.

How It Works:

• Identify a stock or index with low volatility and minimal expected price movement.

• Sell an out-of-the-money (OTM) call and put while buying further OTM options for protection.

Example: Suppose a stock is trading at $100. You could sell a $105 call and a $95 put while buying a $110 call and a $90 put. The maximum profit is achieved if the stock stays between $95 and $105 by expiration.

Why It's Effective for Weeklies:

• Weekly options have accelerated time decay (Theta), which benefits short options.

• The short duration minimizes the impact of unexpected market events.

2. Straddles for Volatility Plays

A Straddle involves buying both a call and a put at the same strike price, making it a powerful strategy for profiting from significant price movements, regardless of direction.

How It Works:

• Choose a stock with an upcoming earnings report or significant news event.

• Buy an ATM (ATM) call and put it with the same expiration.

Example: If a stock trades at $100, you could buy a $100 call and a $100 put. If the stock moves significantly above or below $100, the gains from one leg will offset the losses from the other.

Why It's Effective for Weeklies:

- Weekly options are often cheaper than monthly options, reducing the cost of the Straddle.

- Significant price movements within a short timeframe can lead to substantial profits.

3. Calendar Spreads for Earnings Events

Calendar Spreads involve selling a short-term option and buying a longer-term option at the same strike price. This strategy is particularly effective for trading weekly options around earnings announcements.

How It Works:

- Identify a stock with an upcoming earnings report.

- Sell a weekly option and buy a monthly option at the same strike price.

Example: If a stock is trading at $100, you could sell a $100 call expiring this week and buy a $100 call expiring next month—the strategy profits from the weekly option's time decay.

Why It's Effective for Weeklies:

- Weekly options experience rapid time decay, benefiting the spread's sold leg.

- Implied volatility often spikes before earnings, creating profit opportunities.

4. Scalping Weekly Options for Quick Gains

Scalping involves making multiple small trades to capture quick profits. This strategy works well with weekly options due to their high sensitivity to price movements (Delta).

How It Works:

- Use technical indicators like moving averages or RSI to identify short-term price trends.
- Enter and exit positions quickly to lock in gains.

For example, buy a weekly call option if a stock's price exceeds a key resistance level. Exit the trade when the stock shows sign of consolidation or reversal.

Why It's Effective for Weeklies:

- Weekly options' high Delta provides greater leverage for small price movements.
- Short holding periods reduce exposure to time decay.

Overcoming Weekly Trading Challenges

While weekly options offer significant profit potential, they also have unique challenges. Understanding and addressing these challenges is critical for long-term success.

1. Managing Rapid Time Decay

Time decay (Theta) accelerates as options approach expiration, making weekly options susceptible to the passage of time.

Solution:

- Use strategies that benefit from time decay, such as Iron Condors or credit spreads.

- Avoid extending options until expiration unless the underlying asset moves significantly in your favor.

2. Dealing with High Volatility

Weekly options are often associated with higher implied volatility, especially before major events like earnings reports.

Solution:

- Use volatility-neutral strategies, such as Iron Condors or Calendar Spreads, to mitigate risk.

- Monitor implied volatility levels and adjust your strategy accordingly.

3. Avoiding Overtrading

The short duration of weekly options can tempt traders to overtrade, leading to increased transaction costs and emotional decision-making.

Solution:

- Stick to a well-defined trading plan and avoid impulsive trades.

- Focus on quality setups rather than chasing every opportunity.

4. Minimizing Execution Risk

The tight timeframes of weekly options require precise execution to maximize profitability.

Solution:

•   Use limit orders instead of market orders to control entry and exit prices.

•   Monitor liquidity to ensure tight bid-ask spreads and avoid slippage.

5. Handling Psychological Pressure

The fast pace of weekly options trading can create significant stress, especially for beginners.

Solution:

•   Start with small position sizes to reduce emotional pressure.

•   Focus on the process rather than the outcome, and treat each trade as a learning experience.

Practical Tips for Weekly Options Trading

1.   Leverage Technology:

•   Use trading platforms with advanced charting and real-time data to identify opportunities quickly.

2.   Focus on High-Liquidity Options:

•   Trade options on stocks or indices with high volume to ensure smooth execution and tight spreads.

3. Stay Informed:

• Monitor economic calendars and news events to anticipate market movements.

4. Diversify Strategies:

• Combine different strategies, such as Iron Condors and Straddles, to adapt to varying market conditions.

5. Track Your Performance:

• Maintain a trading journal to analyze your successes and mistakes, helping you refine your approach over time.

Conclusion

Weekly options offer traders a unique opportunity to capitalize on short-term market movements. By combining strategies such as Iron Condors, Straddles, Calendar Spreads, and Scalping, traders can maximize their gains while managing risk effectively. However, success requires a thorough understanding of the challenges posed by weekly options, including rapid time decay, high volatility, and execution risks.

By addressing these challenges and following best practices, you can harness the power of weekly options to enhance your trading performance. With discipline, preparation, and continuous learning, weekly options can become a valuable addition to your trading toolkit.

Chapter 14: The Psychology of Long-Term Success

Trading is often compared to a marathon, not a sprint. While short-term wins can be exhilarating, true success in trading requires maintaining discipline and adaptability over the years. The psychological resilience to handle market fluctuations, stay disciplined, and adjust to ever-changing market trends separates long-term successful traders from those who burn out. This chapter explores strategies for keeping discipline over the long haul and adapting effectively to evolving market trends.

Keeping Discipline Over the Years

Discipline is the cornerstone of consistent trading success. However, maintaining it over the years can be challenging, especially during drawdowns or market uncertainty. Below are strategies to help you cultivate and sustain trading discipline over the long term:

1. Stick to a Trading Plan

A well-structured trading plan serves as your roadmap, ensuring consistency in your decisions and reducing emotional trading.

How to Develop Discipline with Your Plan?

- Set clear rules for entry, exit, and position sizing.
- Review and refine your plan periodically to align with market changes.

- Avoid deviating from your plan, even when tempted by "quick opportunities."

2. Focus on the Process, Not the Outcome

Traders often get fixated on the results of individual trades, leading to emotional highs and lows. Instead, focus on consistently executing your strategy.

Key Practices:

- Treat each trade as part of a more extensive system.
- Understand that losses are part of trading and don't define your overall success.
- Celebrate disciplined execution rather than just profitable trades.

3. Maintain Emotional Balance

Emotional trading, driven by fear or greed, is one of the biggest threats to long-term success. Over time, emotions can erode discipline and lead to irrational decisions.

How to Stay Emotionally Balanced:

- Use meditation or mindfulness techniques to stay calm during volatile periods.
- Take breaks from trading when feeling overwhelmed.
- Keep a journal to document your emotional state alongside your trades. This can help you identify patterns and improve self-awareness.

4. Set Realistic Goals

Unrealistic expectations can lead to frustration and reckless behavior. Set attainable goals that align with your trading style and market conditions.

Practical Goal-Setting Tips:

• Focus on consistent monthly or yearly returns rather than unrealistic daily targets.

• Avoid comparing your performance to other traders; focus on your progress.

• Measure success by your ability to follow your strategy, not just monetary gains.

5. Build Resilience Through Reflection

Long-term success requires learning from both wins and losses. Reflection helps you improve and build mental toughness.

Effective Reflection Practices:

• Review your trading journal regularly to identify areas for improvement.

• Analyze your biggest mistakes and successes to extract valuable lessons.

• Develop a growth mindset, viewing setbacks as opportunities to learn.

6. Avoid Burnout

Trading can be mentally exhausting, especially during prolonged market uncertainty or drawdowns. Preventing burnout is crucial for maintaining discipline over the years.

How to Prevent Burnout:

• Take regular breaks to recharge.

• Diversify your interests and hobbies outside of trading.

• Set boundaries for your trading hours to maintain a healthy work-life balance.

Adapting to Market Trends

Markets are dynamic and constantly evolving. Strategies that worked in one market environment may become obsolete in another. Successful traders must remain adaptable and open to change.

1. Stay Informed About Market Changes

Keeping up with economic, political, and technological developments can help you anticipate shifts in market behavior.

How to Stay Updated:

• Follow reputable financial news sources and reports.

• Study historical market trends to understand how similar events impacted the markets.

• Participate in trading communities to gain diverse perspectives.

2. Learn to Identify Market Phases

Markets cycle through different phases, including trending, consolidating, and volatile conditions. Adapting your strategies to each phase is crucial for long-term success.

How to Adapt to Market Phases:

• Use technical indicators like moving averages or RSI to identify trends or consolidations.

• Switch to trend-following strategies during trending markets and mean-reversion strategies during consolidation periods.

• Scale back your trading during highly volatile periods if your strategy is not suited to such conditions.

3. Incorporate New Tools and Techniques

Technology and innovation continually introduce new tools to improve trading efficiency and accuracy. Staying open to these advancements can give you an edge.

Examples of Useful Tools:

• Algorithmic trading platforms to automate strategies.

• Advanced charting software for improved technical analysis.

• Machine learning models to analyze large datasets and predict market trends.

4. Expand Your Knowledge Base

Long-term success requires continuous learning. Markets evolve, and staying ahead means expanding your understanding of new trading techniques and theories.

Ways to Keep Learning:

• Attend webinars, conferences, and workshops hosted by experienced traders.

• Enroll in advanced trading courses to deepen your expertise.

• Read books and whitepapers on emerging financial technologies, such as blockchain and AI in trading.

5. Test and Evolve Your Strategies

Regularly backtesting and refining your strategies ensures they remain effective in changing markets.

Steps to Test and Evolve:

• Use historical data to test how your strategy performs in different market conditions.

• Make incremental changes rather than overhauling your strategy entirely.

• Document your findings and adjust your trading plan accordingly.

6. Diversify Your Portfolio

Markets are interconnected, and relying too heavily on a single asset class can increase risk. Diversification allows you to adapt to market changes without overexposing yourself.

Diversification Tips:

• Trade across asset classes, such as stocks, options, forex, and commodities.

• Consider geographic diversification by trading international markets.

• Allocate a portion of your portfolio to longer-term investments to balance short-term trading risks.

7. Embrace Flexibility

Rigidly sticking to a single approach can hinder your ability to capitalize on new opportunities. Flexibility ensures you can pivot when needed.

How to Be Flexible:

• Maintain an open mindset and be willing to experiment with new strategies.

• Be prepared to exit trades or strategies that no longer align with market conditions.

• Adjust your risk tolerance based on market volatility and personal financial goals.

Conclusion

The psychology of long-term success in trading requires a balance of discipline and adaptability. Staying disciplined over the years ensures consistency and helps you weather the inevitable ups and downs of trading. At the same time, adapting to market trends allows you to stay relevant and competitive in an ever-changing environment.

By focusing on process over outcomes, maintaining emotional balance, and embracing continuous learning, you can build a resilient mindset capable of thriving in the long term. Remember, success in trading is not about perfection but persistence and growth. With the right psychological approach, you can navigate the trading challenges and achieve sustainable success.

Chapter 15: Avoiding Overtrading and Missteps

Trading can be exhilarating, but it's easy to let emotions and impatience push you into overtrading or making costly mistakes. While ambition is essential for growth, overtrading can quickly erode your account, lead to burnout, and derail your long-term success. This chapter will explore how to recognize overtrading risks and the key lessons traders can learn from failed trades.

Recognizing Overtrading Risks

Overtrading is one of the most common pitfalls for traders. It occurs when you place too many trades in a short period, often without sufficient analysis or a clear rationale. This behavior is driven by various factors, including emotional reactions, greed, or the fear of missing out (FOMO). Recognizing and addressing these risks is critical for protecting your account and maintaining discipline.

1. Understanding the Causes of Overtrading

Overtrading can stem from several psychological and situational triggers:

• **Chasing Losses:** After a losing trade, some traders double down or open new trades to recover quickly. This impulsive behavior often leads to even more significant losses.

- **FOMO (Fear of Missing Out):** Seeing others profit from a market move can tempt traders to jump in without proper analysis or preparation.

- **Greed:** After a successful trade, the desire for more profit can lead to overconfidence and unnecessary risk-taking.

- **Boredom:** Traders who do not follow a structured plan may need to trade constantly, even when market conditions don't support their strategy.

- **Lack of Patience:** Impatience can cause traders to deviate from their plan, entering trades prematurely or overleveraging positions.

2. Identifying the Signs of Overtrading

Recognizing the symptoms of overtrading is the first step to addressing it:

- **Excessive Transactions:** Placing trades far more frequently than your trading plan allows.

- **High Transaction Costs:** Realizing that fees and commissions are eating into your profits due to frequent trades.

- **Emotional Fatigue:** Feeling stressed, frustrated, or anxious after trading sessions.

- **Diminishing Returns:** Noticing that your trades are less profitable or consistently losing money due to impulsive decisions.

3. How to Prevent Overtrading

To combat overtrading, implement the following strategies:

• **Stick to a Trading Plan:** Outline specific trade entries, exits, and position size rules. Follow this plan rigorously to avoid impulsive decisions.

• **Set Daily Limits:** Establish a maximum number of trades or a daily loss limit. Stop trading once you've reached these thresholds.

• **Focus on Quality Over Quantity:** Prioritize high-probability setups rather than trading every market movement.

• **Take Breaks.** When emotions start to take over, step away from your screen. A clear mind leads to better decisions.

• **Review Your Performance:** Keep a trading journal to track your trades and identify patterns of overtrading.

Key Lessons from Failed Trades

Every trader experiences failed trades. While losses are inevitable, they are also growth opportunities. The key is to analyze your mistakes, learn from them, and adjust your approach accordingly. Below are some of the most important lessons to take away from failed trades:

1. The Importance of Risk Management

One of the most common causes of failed trades is poor risk management. Traders who risk too much on a single trade or fail to use stop-loss orders often suffer significant losses.

Lesson: Always define your risk before entering a trade. A general rule of thumb is to risk no more than 1-2% of your account on any single position. Use stop-loss orders to limit potential losses and protect your capital.

2. Patience Pays Off

Rushing into trades without waiting for confirmation signals can lead to unnecessary losses. Many failed trades occur because traders act on incomplete or unreliable information.

Lesson: Be patient and wait for your setup to align with your trading strategy. Entering trades too early or chasing market movements often results in poor outcomes.

3. Emotional Trading Leads to Mistakes

Emotions such as fear, greed, and frustration can cloud judgment and lead to irrational decisions. Emotional trading often causes traders to deviate from their plans or hold onto losing positions for too long.

Lesson: Develop emotional discipline by focusing on the process rather than the outcome of individual trades. Use techniques like meditation or mindfulness to stay calm and centered during volatile markets.

4. Adaptability Is Key

Market conditions are constantly changing. Strategies that worked in one environment may fail in another. Stubbornly sticking to a single approach without adapting can lead to repeated losses.

Lesson: Regularly review and refine your strategies to ensure they remain effective in changing market conditions. Stay informed about economic events and market trends that could impact your trades.

5. Overconfidence Can Be Dangerous

After a series of successful trades, it's easy to become overconfident and take excessive risks. This mindset often leads to significant losses when the market moves against you.

Lesson: Stay humble and grounded, regardless of your recent performance. Treat every trade with the same level of caution and analysis, regardless of past successes.

6. Analyze Your Mistakes Objectively

Many traders fail to learn from their mistakes because they don't analyze their trades objectively. Instead, they blame external factors or avoid reviewing their losses altogether.

Lesson: Use a trading journal to document your trades, including your rationale, execution, and outcomes. Review failed trades to identify patterns and areas for improvement. This practice will help you avoid repeating the same mistakes.

Practical Steps to Avoid Repeating Mistakes

1.   Set Clear Goals: Define and align your trading objectives with your strategies. Having clear goals keeps you focused and prevents impulsive decisions.

2.   Use Technology: Leverage tools like alerts, automated stop-loss orders, and risk calculators to enforce discipline and minimize human error.

3.   Learn from Other Traders: Join trading communities or study the experiences of successful traders. Their insights can help you avoid common pitfalls.

4.   Take Responsibility. Accept full responsibility for your trades, whether they succeed or fail. Blaming external factors will only hinder your growth.

5.   Stay Educated: Continuously expand your knowledge through books, courses, and market analysis. The more you learn, the better equipped you'll be to handle challeng

6.   Focus on Long-Term Success: Avoid the temptation to chase quick profits. Instead, prioritize consistent, sustainable growth over time.

Conclusion

Avoiding overtrading and learning from failed trades are essential skills for achieving long-term success in trading. By recognizing the risks of overtrading and implementing strategies to prevent it, you can protect your account and maintain discipline. Additionally, analyzing failed trades objectively and extracting valuable lessons from them will help you refine your approach and build resilience.

Remember, trading is as much a psychological endeavor as a technical one. By staying patient, disciplined, and adaptable, you can navigate the trading challenges and position yourself for sustainable success. Mistakes are inevitable, but how you respond to them will determine your ultimate trajectory as a trader.

Chapter 16: Essential Rules for Options Trading

Options trading can be advantageous but also highly complex and risky. To navigate this world successfully, traders need guiding principles to remain profitable and manage emotional decisions. This chapter focuses on the essential rules every trader should follow to stay profitable and keep emotions in check.

Rules for Staying Profitable

Profitability in options trading isn't just about making the right trades; it's about having the right mindset and approach. Adhering to these rules can maximize your chances of long-term success.

1. Always Have a Plan

Profitable trading begins with a detailed trading plan. Without one, you're more likely to make impulsive and inconsistent decisions.

What to Include in Your Plan:

• Entry and Exit Rules: Define the conditions for entering and exiting a trade.

• Risk Management: Determine the percentage of your account you're willing to risk per trade (typically 1-2%).

- Profit Targets: Set realistic profit goals to maintain discipline.

- Strategy: Specify whether you use spreads, straddles, covered calls, or other techniques.

2. Focus on Risk-Reward Ratios

A solid risk-reward ratio ensures that you can remain profitable even if you lose more trades than you win.

The Rule:

- Aim for a minimum risk-reward ratio of 1:2. You potentially risk $1 to gain $2.

Why It Works:

- With a 1:2 ratio, you only need to win 34% of your trades to break even.

- It protects your capital during losing streaks.

3. Never Risk More Than You Can Afford to Lose

Options trading can wipe out accounts quickly if not approached cautiously.

The Rule:

- Never risk more than 1-2% of your total account value on a single trade.

Why It Matters:

- This rule ensures that even losses won't decimate your account.

- More minor risks provide the psychological cushion to trade with confidence.

4. Use Stop-Loss Orders

Stop-loss orders are essential for minimizing losses and protecting your capital.

The Rule:

- Always set a stop-loss level when entering a trade.

- Base your stop-loss on technical analysis or your risk tolerance.

Example: If you buy a call option for $2.00, you might set your stop-loss at $1.00 to limit your loss to 50% of the premium paid.

5. Avoid Overleveraging

Leverage can amplify both profits and losses, making it a double-edged sword.

The Rule:

- Use leverage sparingly and understand its implications.

- Avoid using more than 2-3 times your account size in leveraged trades.

Why It's Important:

- Overleveraging can lead to massive losses during market volatility.

- Focusing on consistent, smaller gains is better than chasing big wins.

6. Master One Strategy at a Time

Options trading offers countless strategies, but trying to master them all at once can dilute your effectiveness.

The Rule:

- Focus on one strategy, such as covered calls or credit spreads, and master it before moving on to others.

Why It Helps:

- Specialization allows you to refine your approach and build confidence.

- You'll better understand the nuances of a single strategy, improving your success rate.

7. Analyze Your Trades

Consistent profitability requires reviewing and learning from past trades.

The Rule:

- Keep a detailed trading journal that records the rationale, execution, and outcome of each trade.

Benefits:

- Identifies patterns in your successes and failures.
- It helps refine your strategies over time.

Rules for Managing Emotional Decisions

Emotions are one of the biggest challenges in trading. Fear, greed, and frustration can lead to impulsive decisions and significant losses. These rules will help you maintain emotional control.

1. Detach Emotionally from Your Trades

Every trade should be based on logic and analysis, not emotions.

The Rule:

- View trading as a numbers game with probabilities, not certainties.
- Avoid becoming emotionally attached to any single trade.

How to Achieve It:

- Focus on the process, not individual outcomes.
- Accept losses as part of the game and move on.

2. Avoid Revenge Trading

Revenge trading occurs when traders try to recover losses by immediately entering another trade, often without proper analysis.

The Rule:

- Take a break after a losing trade to regain emotional balance.

- Stick to your trading plan, regardless of recent outcomes.

Why It Matters:

- Impulsive trades made out of frustration often lead to more significant losses.

3. Set Realistic Expectations

Unrealistic expectations can lead to disappointment, frustration, and poor decision-making.

The Rule:

- Aim for steady, consistent gains rather than chasing massive profits.

- Understand that not every trade will be a winner.

Why It Helps:

- Realistic expectations reduce emotional pressure and help you stay disciplined.

- You'll focus on long-term growth rather than short-term gratification.

4. Follow a Routine

A structured routine helps eliminate impulsive decisions and keeps you focused on your strategy.

The Rule:

- Start each trading day with a review of your plan and market analysis.

- Avoid deviating from your routine, even during volatile markets.

Benefits:

- A routine reinforces discipline and reduces emotional reactions.

- It ensures you approach each trade with a clear mind.

5. Use Technology to Remove Emotion

Modern trading platforms offer tools that help automate decision-making and reduce emotional involvement.

The Rule:

- Use stop-loss and take-profit orders to automate exits.

- Set alerts for key price levels to avoid over-monitoring trades.

Why It Works:

- Automation eliminates the need for emotional decisions during high-pressure situations.

- Alerts and orders keep you focused on your strategy.

6. Take Breaks During Emotional Highs and Lows

Trading during periods of heightened emotion can lead to poor judgment.

The Rule:

• Step away from your screen if you feel overly excited or frustrated.

• Take regular breaks to maintain focus and clarity.

Why It Helps:

• Breaks prevent burnout and allow you to approach the market with a fresh perspective.

• They reduce the likelihood of emotional, impulsive trades.

7. Celebrate Discipline, Not Just Profits

Focusing solely on profits can create unnecessary pressure and lead to emotional swings.

The Rule:

• Reward yourself for following your plan, regardless of the trade outcome.

• Measure success by your ability to execute consistently, not by individual wins or losses.

Why It Matters:

• Celebrating discipline reinforces good habits.

• It helps you stay grounded and focused on long-term success.

Conclusion

The essential rules for options trading are designed to help traders stay profitable and manage emotional decisions effectively. By adhering to principles such as risk management, focusing on a single strategy, and automating processes, you can build a strong foundation for consistent trading success. At the same time, emotional control is equally critical, as fear, greed, and frustration can derail even the most well-thought-out plans.

By combining discipline with a structured approach, you can navigate the complexities of options trading with confidence and resilience. Remember, long-term success is not entirely avoiding losses but managing them effectively and continuously improving your strategy. With these rules in place, you're well-equipped to thrive in the dynamic world of options trading.

Chapter 17: Advanced Insights from the Greeks

Options trading becomes significantly more nuanced when traders dive deeper into the Greeks—Delta, Gamma, Theta, Vega, and Rho. While basic understanding helps formulate trades, advanced applications of Vega and Theta provide the edge needed to optimize strategies and manage risk effectively. This chapter explores the more profound implications of Vega and Theta. It explains how to adjust strategies based on various risk profiles.

More profound Applications of Vega and Theta

Understanding Vega in Advanced Contexts

Vega measures an option's sensitivity to changes in implied volatility (IV). Traders often overlook Vega, but it is critical to evaluate options, especially during significant market uncertainty or upcoming events such as earnings announcements.

Key Insights About Vega:

1.   **Vega and Event-Driven Strategies:**

•   Vega spikes before anticipated market events (e.g., earnings report or economic data releases).

- Traders can use this knowledge to execute strategies such as buying straddles or strangles ahead of events to profit from rising IV.

- Conversely, implied volatility typically drops after the event—a phenomenon known as the "volatility crush." This provides an opportunity to sell options and profit from Vega's decay.

2. **Example:** A trader expects significant volatility for a stock before its earnings announcement. They purchase a straddle (buying both a call and a put) to benefit from the anticipated IV increase. After the announcement, they close the position to avoid losses from the post-event IV collapse.

3. **Vega and Long-Term Options (LEAPS):**

- Long-term options, or LEAPS (Long-term Equity Anticipation Securities), have higher Vega than short-term options.

- This means LEAPS are more sensitive to changes in IV, making them ideal for traders expecting sustained volatility over extended periods.

4. **Application:** Traders can use LEAPS to hedge long-term portfolio positions, benefiting from increases in volatility while maintaining directional flexibility.

5. **Vega Neutral Strategies:**

• Advanced traders employ Vega-neutral strategies to isolate directional risk or Theta decay. These strategies involve balancing positions so that changes in Vega do not significantly affect the overall portfolio.

• Examples include combining long and short options or using spreads to offset Vega exposure.

6. Why It Matters: Vega-neutral strategies benefit volatile markets, where sudden spikes or drops in IV can impact profitability.

Advanced Applications of Theta

Theta measures the rate at which an option loses value as expiration approaches. While many traders associate Theta with risk (as it erodes the value of extended possibilities), it can also be a powerful ally in income-generating strategies.

Key Insights About Theta:

1. Maximizing Theta in Short-Term Options:

• Theta decay accelerates as expiration nears. Traders selling weekly or monthly options can benefit from this rapid time decay.

• Popular strategies include selling covered calls or cash-secured puts.

2. Example: A trader sells a weekly call option on a stock they own, generating consistent income as Theta erodes the option's value.

3. Theta and Low-Volatility Markets:

• Theta strategies, such as Iron Condors or credit spreads, perform well in low-volatility markets where price movement is limited.

• Traders collect premiums while the underlying asset remains range-bound, maximizing profits from time decay.

4. Minimizing Theta Risk in Long Options:

• Long option holders must carefully account for Theta risk by timing entries and exits.

• Holding an option too close to expiration without significant movement in the underlying asset can result in a total loss.

5. Mitigation Strategies:

• Roll positions to later expirations to reset Theta decay.

• Use spreads (e.g., vertical spreads) to offset some of the Theta risk while retaining directional exposure.

6. Theta Scalping:

• Traders employ Theta scalping by selling short-term options while carefully managing directional risk.

• This approach requires frequent adjustments but can yield steady returns in stable markets.

Adjusting Strategies Based on Risk Profiles

Options trading isn't a one-size-fits-all endeavor. Every trader has a unique risk tolerance and financial goal. By tailoring strategies to align with individual risk profiles, traders can optimize their approach and mitigate potential losses.

1. Conservative Traders

Conservative traders prioritize capital preservation and steady income over high-risk, high-reward trades.

Recommended Strategies:

• **Covered Calls:** Generate income by selling call options on stocks already owned.

• **Why It Works:** Reduces downside risk while creating a consistent income stream.

• **Cash-Secured Puts:** Sell put options with sufficient cash reserved to purchase the stock if assigned.

• **Why It Works:** Provides an opportunity to acquire stocks at a discount while earning a premium.

• **Iron Condors:** Use this neutral strategy to profit from range-bound markets with minimal risk.

2. Moderate Risk Takers

Traders with a moderate risk appetite aim to balance income and growth.

Recommended Strategies:

- **Vertical Spreads:** Combine long and short options at different strike prices to reduce risk while retaining upside potential.

- **Example:** A bull call spread involves buying a lower strike call and selling a higher one, limiting risk and reward.

- **Calendar Spreads:** Profit from time decay and IV changes by selling short-term options and buying long-term options at the same strike price.

- **Straddles or Strangles:** These strategies allow you to capitalize on significant price movements while accepting higher initial costs.

3. Aggressive Traders

Aggressive traders seek high returns and are willing to accept more significant risks.

Recommended Strategies:

- **Naked Options:** Selling naked calls or puts can generate substantial income but carries unlimited risk.

- **Caution:** This strategy requires significant capital and should only be used by experienced traders.

- **Ratio Spreads:** Sell multiple options while buying fewer options at a different strike to amplify gains in specific scenarios.

- **LEAPS with Short-Term Options:** Combine long-term directional plays (via LEAPS) with short-term income-generating strategies, such as selling weekly options.

Conclusion

Vega and Theta are the most critical Greeks for advanced options traders. They offer insights into volatility and time decay's impact on trades. By understanding their more profound applications, traders can enhance their strategies, whether hedging portfolios, profiting from event-driven volatility, or generating income through Theta decay.

Additionally, tailoring strategies to align with risk profiles ensures traders maximize returns while staying within their comfort zones. Options trading requires discipline, adaptability, and continuous learning, but mastering these advanced concepts can significantly improve your long-term market success.

Chapter 18: Understanding Market Volatility

Market volatility is one of the most challenging yet rewarding aspects of trading. For many traders, volatile markets can appear unpredictable and intimidating. Still, with the right strategies, volatility can also present incredible profit opportunities. In this chapter, we'll explore how to navigate volatile markets effectively and how to use market volatility to your advantage.

How to Navigate Volatile Markets

Rapid price swings and heightened uncertainty characterize volatile markets. While volatility often accompanies risk, it offers higher potential rewards if managed correctly. Understanding how to navigate these conditions can make the difference between capitalizing on opportunities and falling victim to market turbulence.

1. Understand What Drives Volatility

Market volatility is influenced by several factors, including:

• **Economic Events:** Announcements such as GDP reports, interest rate decisions, and employment data can trigger sharp market movements.

• **Earnings Reports:** Company earnings often lead to significant price fluctuations when results deviate from expectations.

- **Global News:** Geopolitical events, natural disasters, and pandemics can create uncertainty and drive rapid price changes.

- **Market Sentiment:** Fear and greed can amplify volatility as traders react emotionally to news or price trends.

By staying informed about these factors, traders can anticipate periods of heightened volatility and prepare accordingly.

2. Adopt a Risk Management Mindset

Risk management becomes even more critical in volatile markets, where prices can move unpredictably.

Key Risk Management Practices:

- **Use Stop-Loss Orders:** Set predefined exit points to limit potential losses. Adjust stop-loss levels to account for broader price swings in volatile markets.

- **Position Sizing:** Avoid overexposing your account by trading more minor positions. Use position size calculators to determine the appropriate amount of risk per trade.

- **Diversify:** Spread your investments across different asset classes or sectors to reduce the impact of a single market movement.

3. Stick to Your Trading Plan

Volatile markets can tempt traders to act impulsively, deviating from their strategies.

How to Stay Disciplined:

- Review your trading plan before entering the market.
- Avoid chasing trades driven by FOMO (fear of missing out).
- Focus on setups that align with your strategy, even if volatility creates the illusion of endless opportunities.

4. Adapt Your Strategies to Volatility

Some strategies perform better in volatile markets than others. For example:

- A trend-following strategy can capitalize on strong price movements.
- **Breakout strategies** work well when prices breach key support or resistance levels due to increased momentum.
- **Options strategies** like Straddles or Strangles can benefit from heightened implied volatility. They profit from significant price swings in either direction.

5. Monitor Key Indicators

Technical indicators can help traders identify trends and potential reversals in volatile markets. Useful indicators include:

- **Average True Range (ATR):** Measures the average range of price movements, helping traders set stop-loss levels.
- **Bollinger Bands**: Highlight high or low volatility periods and potential breakout points.

- **Volatility Index (VIX):** Known as the "fear gauge," the VIX provides insights into market sentiment and future volatility expectations.

Using Volatility to Your Advantage

While volatility increases risk, it also opens the door to lucrative opportunities. Traders who understand how to harness volatility can turn uncertainty into profit.

1. Trade During Volatile Periods

High volatility creates more opportunities for active traders as prices move significantly within shorter timeframes.

Tips for Profiting During Volatility:

- **Focus on Liquid Markets:** Trade assets with high liquidity to ensure tight spreads and smooth execution.

- **Set Realistic Expectations:** Accept that not every trade will be profitable. Aim for small, consistent wins rather than chasing significant gains.

- **Be Quick to Act:** Use limit orders to secure favorable entry and exit points during rapid price changes.

2. Leverage Options Trading

Options are uniquely suited for volatile markets, as they derive value from price movement and implied volatility.

Strategies to Consider:

- **Buying Straddles or Strangles:** Profit from large price swings in either direction by buying both calls and puts.

- **Selling Credit Spreads:** You can benefit from high premiums by selling options during periods of elevated implied volatility.

- **Using Protective Puts:** Purchase puts for long positions to hedge against downside risk.

3. Embrace Scalping

Scalping involves capturing small profits from rapid price movements. This strategy works well in volatile markets where prices frequently fluctuate.

How to Scalping Effectively:

- Focus on short timeframes (e.g., 1-minute or 5-minute charts).

- Use tight stop-loss orders to minimize risk.

- Prioritize high-probability setups with strong momentum.

4. Capitalize on Overreactions

Due to emotional trading, volatile markets often lead to overreactions, where prices deviate significantly from their intrinsic value.

How to Identify Overreactions:

- Use fundamental analysis to assess whether a stock is undervalued or overvalued after a sharp move.

- Watch for price reversals at key support or resistance levels.

Example: If a stock drops 10% due to panic selling but the underlying fundamentals remain strong, this could be an opportunity to buy at a discount.

5. Utilize Hedging Techniques

Hedging protects your portfolio from adverse price movements during volatile periods.

Common Hedging Methods:

- **Using Inverse ETFs:** Inverse ETFs move in the opposite direction of the market, providing downside protection.

- **Implementing Options:** Buy puts to hedge long positions or sell covered calls to generate income.

6. Follow a "Plan-React" Approach

Volatile markets require a balance between planning and flexibility.

How It Works:

- Have a clear plan for managing trades and risk.

- Stay adaptable and ready to react to sudden changes, such as breaking news or unexpected price movements.

Conclusion

Volatile markets are both a challenge and an opportunity for traders. You can confidently navigate these conditions by understanding what drives volatility and adopting risk management techniques. Additionally, you can turn market turbulence into a profitable advantage by using strategies that capitalize on volatility, such as options trading, scalping, or identifying overreactions.

The key to success lies in preparation, discipline, and adaptability. Approach volatile markets with a clear plan, stay informed and remain flexible. With the right mindset and tools, you can thrive in even the most unpredictable market environments.

Chapter 19: Preparing for Market Changes

Financial markets are dynamic, and changes in economic factors like interest rates or geopolitical events can create uncertainty for traders. Options traders, in particular, need to be prepared for shifts in market conditions, as these changes can significantly impact the pricing and effectiveness of strategies. This chapter will discuss how interest rate changes affect options and explore strategies for navigating unpredictable markets.

How Interest Rate Changes Affect Options

Interest rates are a fundamental driver of financial markets, influencing the cost of borrowing, corporate profitability, and investment flows. For options traders, interest rate changes can directly and indirectly affect options pricing and strategy execution.

1. The Role of Interest Rates in Options Pricing

Interest rates play a role in the Black-Scholes options pricing model, which is used to calculate the fair value of options. One of the components in this model is the "risk-free rate," which is often based on government bond yields.

Impact on Call Options:

• Higher interest rates increase the theoretical value of call options. Call buyers defer the cost of purchasing the underlying asset, and higher rates make this deferral more advantageous.

Impact on Put Options:

• Conversely, higher interest rates decrease the theoretical value of put options. Sellers benefit less from holding cash positions when interest rates rise.

2. Implied Volatility and Interest Rates

Interest rate changes can indirectly influence implied volatility, a key factor in options pricing. When rates rise, market uncertainty may increase, driving implied volatility higher. This can make options more expensive, even if the underlying asset's price remains stable.

3. Strategies for High and Low Interest Rate Environments

Adapting your options strategies to prevailing interest rate conditions is crucial for maintaining profitability:

• High Interest Rate Environments:

• Focus on call options or strategies like covered calls, which benefit from higher call premiums.

• Avoid overleveraging, as higher borrowing costs can reduce your overall profitability.

• Low Interest Rate Environments:

• Consider put options or protective puts to hedge against potential downside risk.

• Explore strategies that rely on tight spreads, as low rates typically coincide with low volatility.

4. Dividend Implications

Higher interest rates can impact dividends, which in turn affect options pricing:

• Stocks with high dividend yields become less attractive in high-rate environments, potentially reducing call premiums.

• Traders should account for dividend changes when calculating options' expected values.

Strategies for Unpredictable Markets

Unpredictable markets are marked by heightened volatility, rapid price movements, and shifting investor sentiment. While these conditions can be challenging, they create opportunities for prepared traders. Below are strategies to navigate such markets effectively.

1. Hedging with Options

Options are inherently designed for risk management, making them an excellent tool for hedging in unpredictable markets.

Hedging Strategies:

• **Protective Puts:** Buy put options to protect long stock positions from downside risk. This strategy ensures a minimum selling price for your shares, regardless of market movements.

• **Collars:** Combine a protective put with a covered call to limit downside risk while generating income from the call premium.

• **Straddles and Strangles:** These strategies involve buying both calls and putting to profit from large price swings in either direction. They are instrumental when you expect high volatility but are uncertain about the direction of the move.

2. Diversifying Your Portfolio

Diversification reduces exposure to a single asset or market, helping to mitigate risks in unpredictable conditions.

How to Diversify:

• Trade across multiple asset classes, such as equities, commodities, and currencies.

• You can gain broad market exposure by using ETFs or index options rather than relying on individual stocks.

• Allocate a portion of your portfolio to non-correlated assets, such as bonds or gold, which perform differently during market downturns.

3. Volatility-Based Strategies

In unpredictable markets, volatility becomes a key driver of options pricing. Traders can capitalize on volatility through the following strategies:

Selling High Volatility:

• Sell options when implied volatility is high to collect higher premiums.

• Strategies like Iron Condors or credit spreads can be effective in range-bound markets with inflated volatility.

Buying Volatility:

• Buy options when you expect a significant increase in volatility. Long straddles and strangles are excellent for this scenario.

4. Using Technical Analysis for Entry and Exit

Technical analysis can provide valuable insights into price patterns and trends, helping traders time their entries and exits in volatile markets.

Key Indicators for Unpredictable Markets:

• **Bollinger Bands:** Identify periods of high or low volatility and potential breakout points.

• **Relative Strength Index (RSI):** Detect overbought or oversold conditions to anticipate reversals.

• **Moving Averages:** Use short- and long-term moving averages to identify trends and crossovers.

5. Adapting Position Sizes

In unpredictable markets, managing position sizes becomes critical for minimizing risk. More prominent positions can amplify losses during sudden price swings.

How to Adjust:

• Reduce your position sizes to lower your overall exposure.

• Allocate a smaller percentage of your account to each trade, ensuring no loss significantly impacts your capital.

6. Remain Emotionally Disciplined

Unpredictable markets can evoke emotions like fear and greed, leading to impulsive decisions.

Tips for Emotional Discipline:

• Stick to your trading plan, regardless of market noise.

• Use stop-loss and take-profit orders to automate your decisions.

• Take breaks during high-stress periods to maintain a clear mindset.

Conclusion

Preparing for market changes is an essential skill for options traders. Interest rate shifts can directly impact options pricing, making understanding their effects on call and put values essential. Tailoring your strategies to high—or low-interest-rate environments can mitigate risks and maximize returns.

In unpredictable markets, hedging, diversification, and volatility-based approaches enable traders to navigate uncertainty effectively. Remaining disciplined and adaptable is key to thriving in these conditions. By understanding the interplay between market changes and options strategies, you can position yourself for success in any market environment.

Chapter 20: Building a Long-Term Trading Career

Options trading is an exciting and potentially lucrative field. However, achieving long-term success requires more than just understanding strategies and market dynamics. It demands a clear roadmap and consistent habits that foster discipline, learning, and financial growth. This chapter explores the blueprint for a successful options trading career and the habits you need to sustain wealth over the years.

The Roadmap to a Successful Options Career

Success in options trading does not happen overnight. It's a journey that requires planning, preparation, and consistent execution. Here is a step-by-step roadmap to guide you toward a thriving career in options trading.

1. Start with Education

Knowledge is the foundation of a successful trading career. Before entering the options market, fully grasp the basics and advanced concepts.

How to Educate Yourself:

• Read foundational books such as "Options as a Strategic Investment" by Lawrence McMillan.

• Take online courses that cover options strategies, risk management, and market analysis.

• Use simulation platforms or paper trading to practice without risking real money.

Why It's Important: Education reduces the likelihood of costly mistakes and builds confidence in your decision-making abilities.

2. Define Your Goals

Every trader has unique motivations and goals. Defining what you want to achieve in options trading will shape your strategies and approach.

Questions to Ask Yourself:

• Are you trading to supplement your income, build wealth, or achieve financial independence?

• How much time can you dedicate to trading each day or week?

• What is your risk tolerance, and how does it align with your financial goals?

Set SMART Goals:

• **Specific:** Outline precise trading objectives (e.g., earning $1,000 monthly in options income).

• **Measurable:** Track your progress with metrics such as win rates and average returns.

• **Achievable:** Start with realistic targets to build confidence and avoid burnout.

- **Relevant:** Align your goals with your long-term career aspirations.

- **Time-Bound:** Set deadlines to stay accountable.

3. Develop a Trading Plan

A well-structured trading plan is your market roadmap, ensuring consistency and reducing emotional decision-making.

Key Components of a Trading Plan:

- **Strategies:** Define the options strategies you'll use, such as credit spreads, iron condors, or long calls.

- **Risk Management:** Specify how much capital you will risk per trade (e.g., 1-2% of your account).

- **Entry and Exit Rules:** Establish clear criteria for entering and exiting trades.

- **Review Process:** Include a plan for reviewing and refining your strategies.

Benefits of a Trading Plan:

- Provides structure and clarity.

- Prevents impulsive decisions.

- It helps you stay focused during volatile market conditions.

4. Build a Strong Risk Management Framework

Risk management is the cornerstone of a sustainable trading career. Without it, even the most profitable strategies can lead to significant losses.

Risk Management Tips:

- **Position Sizing:** Calculate position sizes based on your account size and stop-loss levels to limit your risk on each trade.
- **Diversification:** Avoid overexposing yourself to a single asset or strategy.
- **Use Stop-Loss Orders:** Protect your capital by setting predefined exit points for losing trades.

Why It Matters: Effective risk management ensures that no loss can wipe out your account, allowing you to recover and continue trading.

5. Leverage Technology and Tools

Modern trading platforms and tools can enhance your efficiency and decision-making.

Recommended Tools:

- **Charting Software:** Use platforms like TradingView or Thinkorswim for technical analysis.
- **Options Calculators:** Analyze risk-reward scenarios and calculate Greeks.
- **Economic Calendars:** Stay informed about key events that may impact volatility.

- **Automation Tools:** Automate routine tasks like placing stop-loss orders or monitoring price levels.

6. Focus on Continuous Learning

The markets are constantly evolving, and so should your skills and knowledge.

How to Stay Ahead:

- Follow industry news and trends to identify new opportunities.
- Attend webinars, seminars, or conferences to network with experienced traders.
- Join online communities where traders share insights and strategies.
- Experiment with new strategies in a simulated environment before implementing them in live markets.

Consistent Habits for Long-Term Wealth

Long-term success in options trading is not just about strategy; it's about cultivating habits that promote consistency, discipline, and financial growth. Here are the key habits successful traders follow to build and sustain wealth.

1. Maintain a Trading Journal

A trading journal is invaluable for tracking your performance, identifying patterns, and improving your strategies.

What to Include in Your Journal:

- Trade details (e.g., entry/exit prices, strike prices, premiums paid/received).
- Rationale for each trade (e.g., technical setup, market conditions).
- Outcomes (e.g., profit/loss, lessons learned).

Benefits:

- Identify strengths and weaknesses in your trading approach.
- Encourages accountability and continuous improvement.

2. Practice Emotional Discipline

Emotions like fear and greed can lead to impulsive decisions and undermine your trading plan.

How to Manage Emotions:

- Stick to your trading plan, regardless of market noise.
- Use automation to remove emotion-driven decisions (e.g., stop-loss orders).
- Take breaks during stressful periods to reset your mindset.
- Focus on long-term goals rather than short-term fluctuations.

3. Stay Organized and Consistent

Consistency is key to building wealth over time. Establish a routine that ensures you approach trading with focus and discipline.

Daily Routine Tips:

• Begin each day with market analysis and a review of your trading plan.

• Set specific hours for trading and stick to them.

• Allocate time for post-trade reviews and journaling.

4. Reinvest Profits Strategically

Reinvesting profits can accelerate account growth, but it's essential to do so strategically.

How to Reinvest:

• Allocate a portion of your profits to increase your trading capital.

• Diversify into other asset classes or income-generating investments.

• Set aside funds for education or tools that enhance your trading skills.

Why It Matters: Reinvesting profits compounds your returns over time, enabling exponential growth.

5. Focus on Health and Well-Being

Trading is mentally and emotionally demanding. Maintaining your health ensures you stay sharp and focused.

Tips for Staying Healthy:

- Take regular breaks to avoid burnout.
- Exercise and maintain a balanced diet to improve focus and reduce stress.
- Practice mindfulness or meditation to enhance emotional control.
- Get enough sleep to ensure optimal decision-making.

6. Review and Adapt Regularly

Markets change, and so should your strategies and habits. Regularly reviewing your performance and adapting to new conditions is essential for long-term success.

Review Process:

- Analyze your trading journal for recurring patterns or mistakes.
- Assess the effectiveness of your strategies in different market conditions.
- Stay open to feedback from mentors or peers.
- Make incremental adjustments to improve performance.

7. Maintain a Growth Mindset

A growth mindset focuses on continuous improvement and learning from successes and failures.

How to Cultivate a Growth Mindset?

- Embrace challenges as opportunities to learn.
- View losses as temporary setbacks rather than permanent failures.
- Celebrate progress, even if it's small.
- Surround yourself with supportive and like-minded individuals who encourage growth.

Conclusion

Building a long-term trading career in options requires more than just market knowledge; it demands discipline, consistency, and continuous improvement. By following a clear roadmap, investing in education, and cultivating habits that promote resilience and adaptability, you can navigate the complexities of the market and achieve lasting success.

Remember, success in options trading is a journey, not a destination. Focus on building a strong foundation, remain patient, and embrace the learning process. With time, dedication, and the right approach, you can create a thriving career that delivers financial rewards and personal fulfillment.

Chapter 21: Wrapping Up and Next Steps

As you conclude this guide, you're now equipped with the knowledge and strategies to embark on a confident trading journey. You've built a strong foundation, from understanding options trading fundamentals to mastering advanced strategies, navigating volatility, and managing emotions. But trading is not a destination—it's a continuous journey that demands growth, adaptation, and learning. This final chapter consolidates your roadmap to becoming a confident trader. It discusses how embracing lifelong learning will ensure your long-term success.

Your Roadmap to Becoming a Confident Trader

Confidence in trading comes not from luck but from preparation, discipline, and consistent execution. Below is a roadmap to help you stay on course as you develop your skills and grow as a trader.

1. Commit to a Trading Plan

The importance of a trading plan cannot be overstated. It serves as your compass, guiding your decisions and helping you avoid impulsive actions.

Key Elements of a Trading Plan:

• **Clear Objectives:** Define your financial goals and trading purpose.

• **Risk Management Rules:** Set guidelines for position sizing, stop-loss levels, and maximum risk per trade.

- **Preferred Strategies:** Specify the strategies you'll use, whether covered calls, credit spreads, or straddles.

- **Review Schedule:** Regularly evaluate your performance and update your plan as needed.

Consistency in following your plan builds discipline and confidence, even during challenging market conditions.

2. Develop Emotional Resilience

Trading is as much a psychological endeavor as it is a technical one. Emotional control is critical to navigating the market's highs and lows.

Steps to Build Emotional Resilience:

- **Stay Detached:** Treat each trade as a small part of a larger plan. Don't let individual wins or losses dictate your emotions.

- **Focus on Process Over Outcomes:** Judge success by how well you executed your strategy, not just by the profit or loss.

- **Take Breaks:** To regain perspective, stop trading during periods of frustration or overexcitement.

3. Master Risk Management

Protecting your capital should always be your top priority. A confident trader knows their limited downside and has strategies to handle losses.

Risk Management Practices:

• Never risk more than 1-2% of your account on a single trade.

• Use stop-loss orders to cap potential losses.

• Diversify your portfolio to reduce exposure to a single asset or sector.

By managing risk effectively, you create a safety net, allowing you to trade clearly and confidently.

4. Start Small and Scale Gradually

Confidence grows with experience. Instead of aiming for big wins early on, focus on small, consistent successes.

How to Start Small:

• Begin with paper trading or a demo account to refine your skills without risking real money.

• Trade small position sizes until you're comfortable with your strategy.

• Scale your trades gradually as your account grows and your confidence increases.

This approach limits your risk and allows you to learn from mistakes without significant financial consequences.

5. Adopt a Continuous Improvement Mindset

Every trade is an opportunity to learn. Whether you win or lose, reviewing your trades will help you refine your strategies and improve over time.

How to Review Your Trades:

• Keep a detailed trading journal that records your rationale, execution, and outcomes.

• Analyze patterns in your successes and failures.

• Adjust your trading plan based on insights gained from your reviews.

The most successful traders view their journey as an ongoing learning process.

6. Leverage Technology and Resources

The trading world constantly evolves, and staying up-to-date with tools and resources will give you an edge.

Recommended Tools:

• **Charting Platforms:** Use tools like TradingView for in-depth technical analysis.

• **Options Analysis Software:** Platforms like Thinkorswim or OptionVue can help evaluate risk-reward scenarios.

• **Economic Calendars:** Stay informed about key market events and announcements.

• **Automated Alerts:** Set alerts to monitor price levels and volatility, ensuring you never miss a key opportunity.

Staying current with technology ensures you remain competitive in the fast-paced trading environment.

Embracing the Journey of Lifelong Learning

While this book has given you the tools to start or enhance your trading career, true success lies in your willingness to keep learning and evolving. The market is dynamic, and adapting to its changes requires a commitment to growth.

1. Stay Informed About Market Trends

Various factors, including economic policies, global events, and technological advancements, influence the financial markets. Staying informed will help you anticipate changes and adjust your strategies accordingly.

How to Stay Updated:

• Follow reputable financial news sources like Bloomberg or CNBC.

• Subscribe to newsletters or podcasts from experienced traders.

• Participate in online forums and trading communities to exchange ideas and insights.

2. Invest in Your Education

Lifelong learning involves continuously expanding your knowledge base and skill set.

Ways to Learn:

• Attend webinars, workshops, or trading expos.

• Enroll in advanced courses that focus on specific aspects of options trading.

• Read books and case studies from successful traders to gain inspiration and practical advice.

3. Experiment with New Strategies

As you gain experience, don't be afraid to explore new strategies that align with your evolving goals and market conditions.

How to Experiment Safely:

• Test new strategies in a demo account before applying them in live markets.

• Start with small position sizes to minimize risk.

• Monitor and evaluate the performance of each strategy over time.

Exploration and experimentation keep your trading approach fresh and adaptive.

4. Find a Mentor or Join a Community

Learning from others who have walked the same path can accelerate your progress and help you avoid common pitfalls.

Benefits of Mentorship and Community:

• Gain insights from experienced traders who can provide guidance and constructive feedback.

- Stay motivated by connecting with like-minded individuals.

- Share your own experiences to contribute to the growth of others.

Communities and mentors provide invaluable support and encouragement throughout your trading journey.

5. Embrace Failures as Learning Opportunities

Losses and mistakes are an inevitable part of trading. Rather than viewing them as setbacks, treat them as opportunities to learn and improve.

How to Learn from Failures:

- Analyze what went wrong and identify how to avoid similar mistakes in the future.

- Focus on the lessons gained rather than the monetary loss.

- Remind yourself that even the most successful traders experience losses.

If you're willing to learn from your failures, every failure brings you one step closer to mastery.

Conclusion

Your journey to becoming a confident trader doesn't end with this book—it begins here. By following the roadmap outlined in this chapter and embracing the principles of lifelong learning, you'll position yourself for long-term success in the dynamic world of options trading.

Remember that confidence comes from preparation, discipline, and persistence. Stay committed to your trading plan, manage your risk diligently, and approach every trade with a mindset of growth and improvement. The market will challenge you, but it will also reward prepared and adaptable people.

Most importantly, enjoy the journey. Trading is about building wealth, personal growth, resilience, and mastery. Embrace the process, stay curious, and strive to be your best trader.

Appendices

Glossary of Options Trading Terms

Understanding the terminology is crucial for navigating the world of options trading. Here's a glossary of key terms to reference as you grow in your trading journey:

• **Call Option:** A contract that gives the holder the right to buy an asset at a specified price before the contract expires.

• **Put Option:** A contract that gives the holder the right to sell an asset at a specified price before the contract expires.

• **Strike Price:** The price at which the underlying asset can be bought or sold when exercising an option.

• **Expiration Date:** The date the option must be exercised or will expire worthless.

• **Premium:** The price paid to purchase an option.

- **Intrinsic Value:** If favorable, the difference between the underlying asset's strike price and the current market price.

- Time Value is the portion of the option's premium attributable to the time remaining until expiration.

- Delta: Measures how much an option's price changes with a $1 change in the underlying asset's price.

- **Theta:** Represents the rate of time decay in the value of an option as it approaches expiration.

- **Vega:** Measures an option's sensitivity to changes in market volatility.

- **Gamma:** Tracks the rate of Delta change over time or as the price of the underlying asset changes.

- **Implied Volatility (IV):** The market forecasts a likely movement in the asset's price.

- **In-the-Money (ITM):** An option with intrinsic value (e.g., a call option where the underlying asset price is above the strike price).

- **Out-of-the-Money (OTM):** An option with no intrinsic value (e.g., a put option where the underlying asset price is above the strike price).

- **At-the-Money (ATM):** An option where the strike price roughly equals the underlying asset's current price.

FAQs for New Traders

1. What is the best strategy for beginners in options trading? To get comfortable with the mechanics of options, beginners should focus on simple strategies like buying calls or puts.

Covered calls are also an excellent way to generate income while limiting risk.

2. How much capital do I need to start trading options? While there's no set minimum, starting with at least $2,000 to $5,000 is recommended for adequate diversification and proper risk management. Ensure that only risk capital is used—money you can afford to lose.

3. How do I choose the right strike price? The choice of strike price depends on your trading goals. If you're looking for safety, choose options closer to being in-the-money (ITM). For higher returns (but with higher risk), consider out-of-the-money (OTM) options.

4. What's the difference between options trading and stock trading? Options trading involves contracts that derive value from the underlying asset. In contrast, stock trading is directly buying and selling company shares. Options provide leverage and flexibility but come with added complexity and risks.

5. How can I manage my emotions while trading? Stick to a solid trading plan and predetermined rules for risk management. Avoid overtrading and take breaks when you feel overwhelmed. Remember, trading discipline is critical for success.

6. Can I trade options with a small account? You can trade options with a small account by focusing on low-cost strategies like buying single options or using spreads to limit risk. Pay close attention to fees and avoid overleveraging.

7. How do I analyze whether an option is a good trade? I look at implied volatility, time to expiration, strike price, and the underlying asset's price trend. I use Greeks like Delta and Theta to evaluate the risk and reward potential.

8. What's the role of volatility in options trading? Volatility significantly impacts option pricing. High volatility increases premiums, making selling options potentially profitable. Low volatility reduces premiums, favoring buyers looking for cheaper contracts.

9. How important is backtesting? Backtesting allows you to test strategies on historical data to gauge their effectiveness. It's essential to validate your trading approach before risking real money.

10. Can I lose more than my initial investment? Yes, especially when selling naked options or using specific advanced strategies. Proper risk management and understanding your strategy are crucial to avoiding significant losses.

Cheat Sheets for Quick Reference

1. Options Trading Strategy Cheat Sheet

• Buying Calls: Use when you anticipate the stock price will rise significantly.

• Buying Puts: Use when you expect the stock price to drop significantly.

• Covered Calls: Sell call options on stocks you already own to generate income.

• Iron Condors: Use in low-volatility markets to profit from stable prices.

• Straddles: Buy a call and put it at the same strike price to profit from significant price movements in either direction.

• Credit Spreads: Sell one option and buy another with a lower premium to generate income while capping risk.

2. Risk Management Cheat Sheet

• Never risk more than 1-2% of your account on a single trade.

• Use stop-loss orders to limit potential losses.

• Always calculate the risk-to-reward ratio before entering a trade (aim for at least 1:2).

• Diversify your trades to spread risk across different assets or strategies.

3. Option Greeks Cheat Sheet

• **Delta:** Measures price sensitivity to the underlying asset. A Delta of 0.5 means the option's price will move $0.50 for every $1 move in the underlying stock.

• **Theta:** Represents time decay. A Theta of -0.05 means the option loses a $0.05 daily value.

- **Vega:** Tracks sensitivity to volatility. A Vega of 0.10 means the option's price will increase $0.10 for every 1% increase in volatility.

- **Gamma:** Measures the change in Delta. High Gamma means Delta changes quickly as the stock price moves.

Key Trading Tools Cheat Sheet

- **Trading Platforms:** ThinkorSwim, Interactive Brokers, and Tastyworks for advanced options trading.

- **Analysis Tools:** Options Profit Calculator, Volatility Rank Tools, and Backtesting Software.

- **Educational Resources:** Books like Options as a Strategic Investment by Lawrence McMillan or online courses on options trading basics.

Using these appendices as a reference allows you to streamline your learning process, avoid common pitfalls, and improve your trading decisions. These resources are designed to serve as your go-to guide while navigating the complex but rewarding world of options trading.

-

Printed in Dunstable, United Kingdom

63947844R00129